AF593449

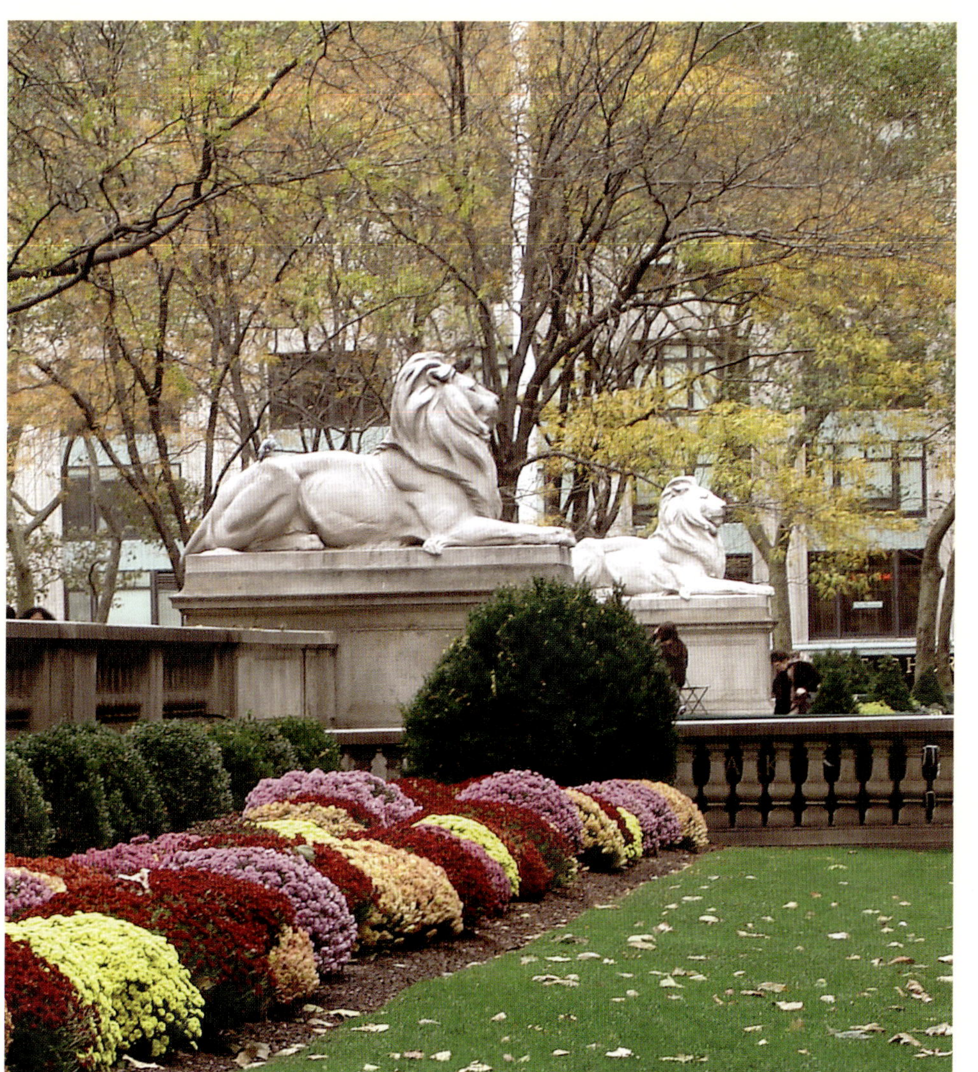

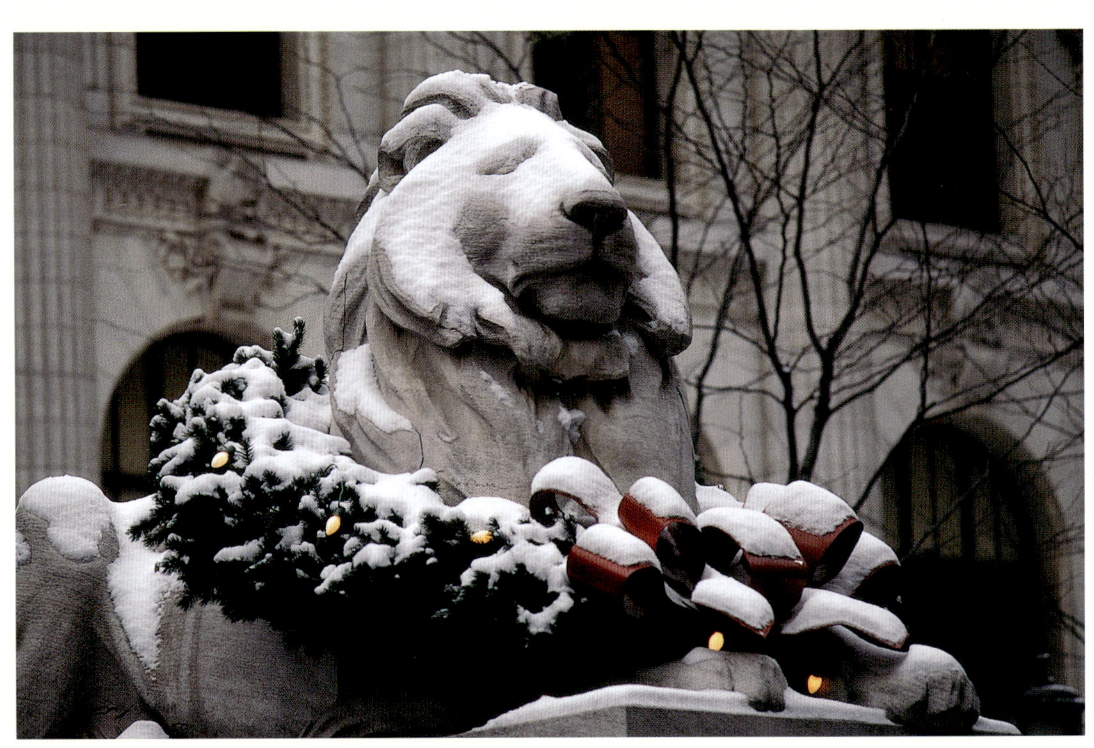

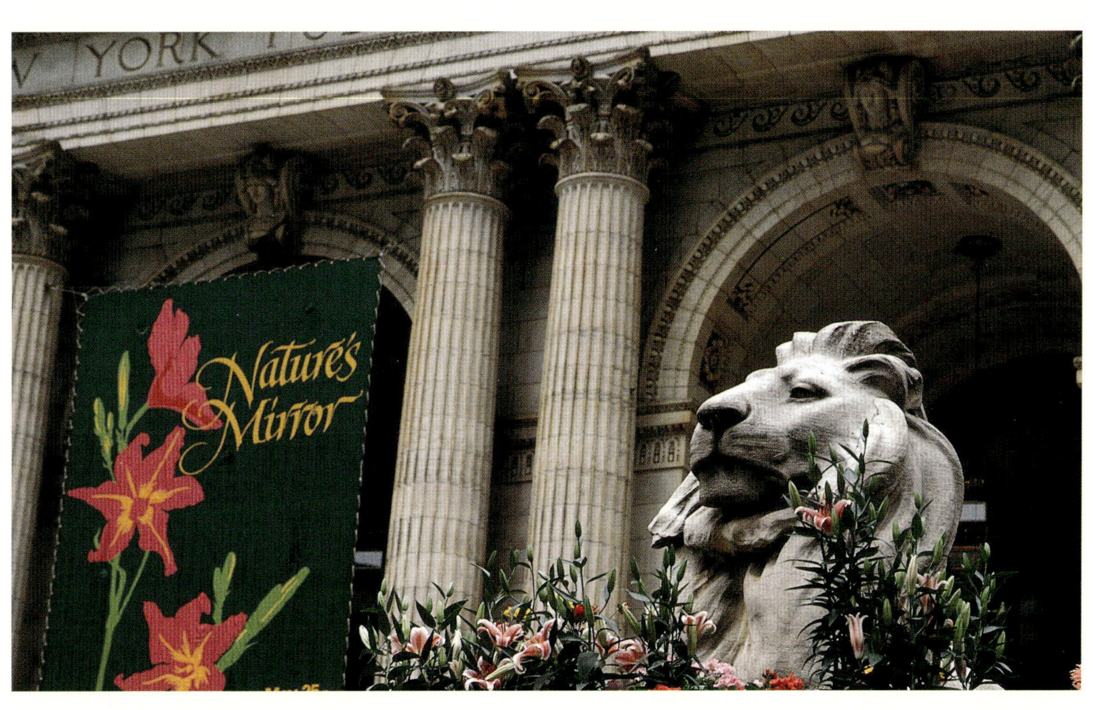
Nature's
Mirror

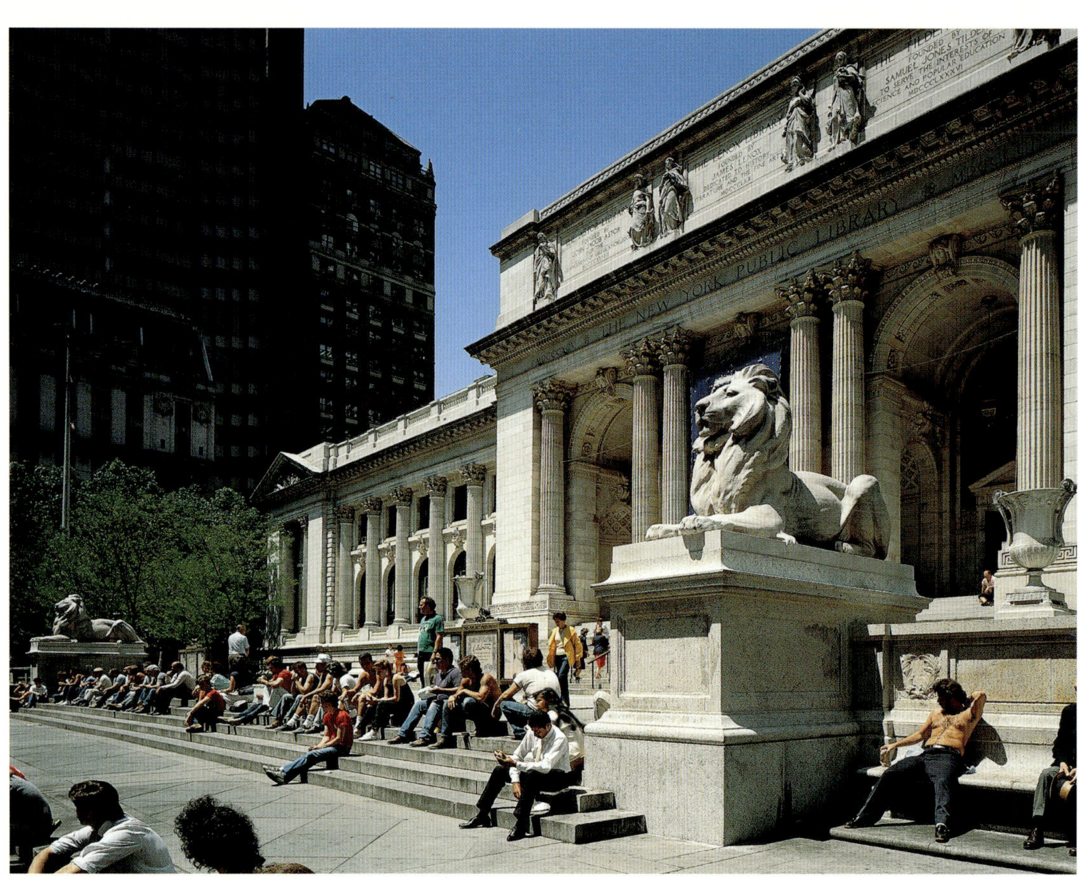
THE NEW YORK PUBLIC LIBRARY
FOUNDED BY
SAMUEL JONES TILDEN
TO SERVE THE INTERESTS OF
SCIENCE AND POPULAR EDUCATION
MDCCCLXXXVI
THE LENOX LIBRARY
FOUNDED BY
JAMES LENOX

Top Cats

The Life and Times of The New York Public Library Lions

SUSAN G. LARKIN

Pomegranate
SAN FRANCISCO

Published by Pomegranate Communications, Inc.
Box 808022, Petaluma CA 94975
800 227 1428 • www.pomegranate.com

Pomegranate Europe Ltd.
Unit 1, Heathcote Business Centre, Hurlbutt Road
Warwick, Warwickshire CV34 6TD, UK
[+44] 0 1926 430111 • sales@pomeurope.co.uk

NYPL Editor and Picture Researcher: Kenneth Benson
NYPL Photographer: Peter Riesett

Special thanks to the NYPL Staff members who helped make *Top Cats* possible: Sara Abraham, Barbara Bergeron, Marc Blaustein, Jeanne Bornstein, Ruth Carr, Alice Dowd, Andrea Felder, Tina Hoerenz, Michael Inman, Maira Liriano, Tom Lisanti, David Lowe, John Lundquist, Samuel Mendez, Lis Pearson, Warren Platt, Lee Robinson, Vincenzo Rutigliano, Stephen Saks, Nicole Simpson, David Smith, William Stingone, Karen Van Westering, Joseph Vissers, and Jennifer Woolf, as well as Jim Moske, former NYPL Archivist.

Jacket design by Lisa Reid
Book design by Barbara Ziller-Caritey

Printed in China

15 14 13 12 11 10 09 08 07 06 10 9 8 7 6 5 4 3 2 1

On the front: A beautifully restored southerly Lion, November 2004.

On the back: The Library Lions in profile, viewed from the south, 1990.

Page 1: The Library Lions set off by a bed of colorful chrysanthemums, October 2005.

Page 2: Lion adorned with a Christmas wreath, 1988.

Page 3: Northerly Lion, with the banner for the exhibition *Nature's Mirror: 200 Years of Botanical Illustration,* May 25–September 2, 1989, in the background.

Page 4: Panoramic view on a summer's day, 1986, of the Fifth Avenue façade of The New York Public Library, stretching two blocks along Fifth Avenue, from 42nd Street to 40th Street.

Pages 9, 46: Plaster cast of the lion mask with ring, modeled by Alexander Phimister Proctor, that was converted into marble for the first-floor window keystones of the Library's façade.

Library of Congress Cataloging-in-Publication data:

Larkin, Susan G., date.
Top cats : the life and times of the New York Public Library lions / Susan G. Larkin.
p. cm.
ISBN 0-7649-3762-6
1. Potter, Edward Clark, 1857–1923. 2. Lions in art. 3. Public sculpture, American—New York (State)—New York. 4. Sculpture—New York (State)—New York. 5. New York Public Library. I. Title.

NB237.P666L37 2006
730.92—dc22

2006043268

Pomegranate Catalog No. A120
ISBN-13: 978-0-7649-3762-0

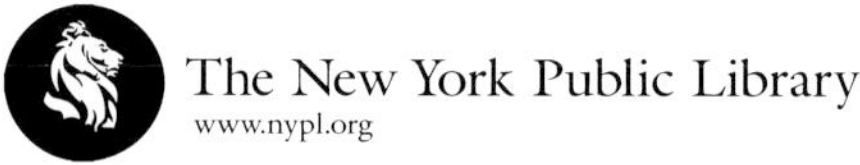

Contents

1. Top Cats: Their Story 8

A Pride of Lions 12

Edward Clark Potter (1857–1923) 16

Sculpting a Marble Monument 24

Lions in the Wild 28

The Piccirilli Brothers 32

What's in a Name? 40

Ensuring a Second Century 44

2. The Lions on Parade 46

The Lions as Fashionable Backdrops 47

Andy and the Lion 50

Feeding the Lions 52

The Lions as Symbols of Libraries and Reading 54

Cartoon Celebrities: *The New Yorker*'s Lions 58

The Lions Adorned 60

On the Cover: *The New Yorker*'s Lions 64

The Lions as Witnesses to History 66

The Lions in Winter 70

The Lions Come to Life 72

Urban Neighbors: The Lions in the City 74

Author's Acknowledgments 77

Further Reading 78

Illustration Credits 80

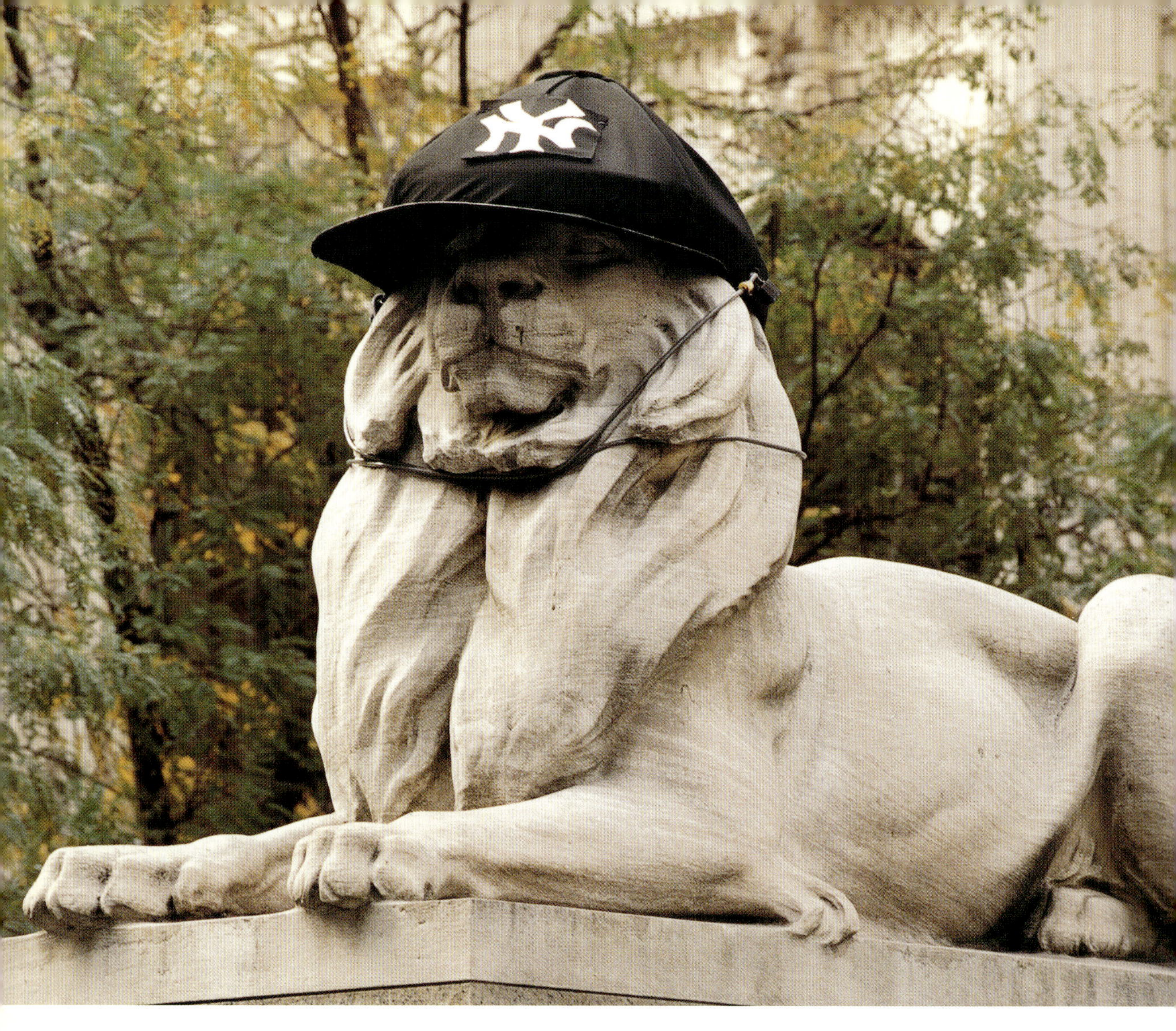

The southerly Lion sported a New York Yankees baseball cap during the Subway Series of 2000. Ensuring impartiality, his uptown brother wore a Mets cap.

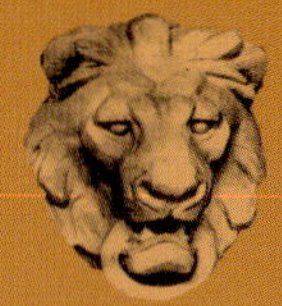

1. Top Cats: Their Story

THE LIONS FLANKING THE GRAND STAIRCASE OUTSIDE THE New York Public Library at Fifth Avenue and 42nd Street are among the best-known and best-loved public sculptures in America. They have been featured in cartoons, children's stories, plays, and movies. In the background of tourist snapshots or television news footage, they communicate instantly that the setting is New York, New York. Adorned with spring flowers, baseball caps, mortarboards, and Christmas wreaths, they have expressed the emotional life of the city. In the decades since they were installed on the plaza overlooking one of Manhattan's busiest intersections, the two marble beasts have been adopted as icons of The New York Public Library, New York City, and libraries in general. What makes them so popular? And why are lions there in the first place?

At the World's Columbian Exposition in Chicago in 1893, a pair of lions by American sculptor Alexander Phimister Proctor flanked the southern entrance to the Palace of Fine Arts (shown here). A similar pair by Edward Kemeys at the northern entrance served as prototypes for his famous cats at the Art Institute of Chicago, unveiled in 1894.

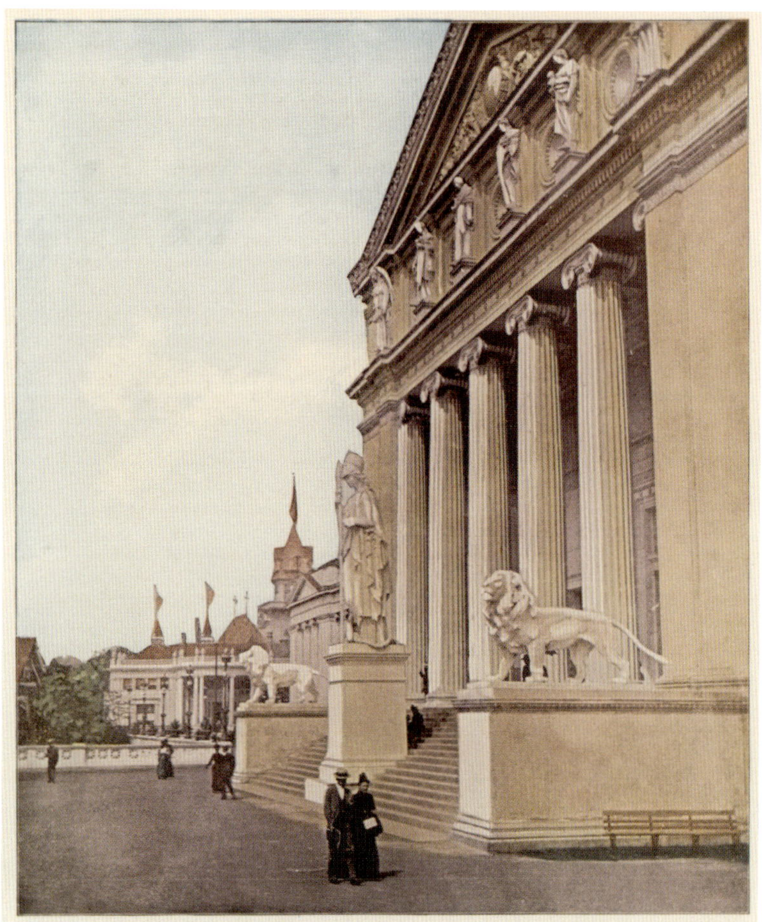

Bronze guardian lion at the Summer Palace, Beijing, late Qing dynasty (1644–1911).

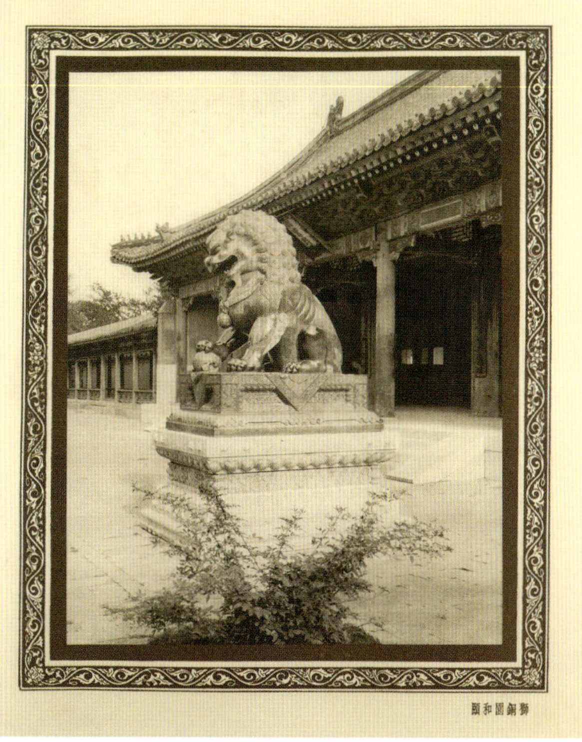

Since ancient times, sculpted lions, often in pairs, have been used at the entrances to public buildings and sacred sites. The Lion Gate at the Hittite stronghold in Boghazkeui, Turkey, dating to ca. 1400 BCE, and the Lioness Gate on the citadel at Mycenae, Greece, ca. 1300–1200 BCE, exemplify the use of lions as guardians of military fortifications, intended to impress and even frighten visitors with the might associated with the animals and, by extension, the inhabitants. That symbolism was not confined to the Western world. Pairs of snarling lions guard the approach to many temples, tombs, and palaces in China. Apart from its ferocity, the lion's nobility as the storied "King of the Beasts" recommends it as an emblem of dignity and power, often expressed in a calm, reclining pose. Renaissance Italy abounded in guardian lions, including a

A Pride of Lions

From the earliest ages, lions have inspired artists. The cave paintings at Chauvet, France, dating to 30,000 BCE, are the oldest known paintings in the world. This detail from the Lion Panel at Chauvet depicts a pride of lions hunting bison.

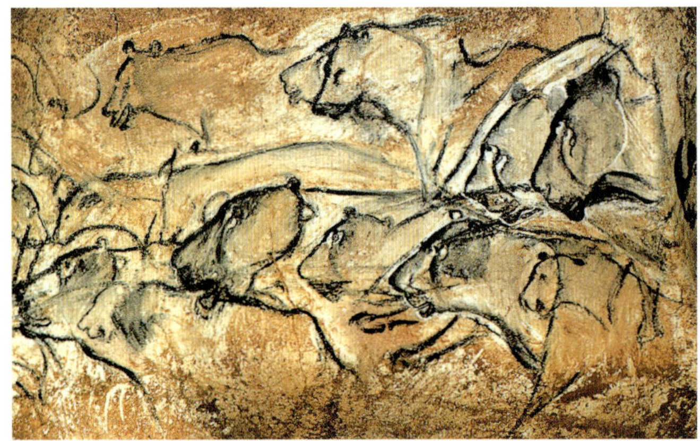

This ferocious lion, a daunting 8½ feet tall, was one of a pair carved ca. 883–859 BCE. The sculptures flanked the entrance to a temple dedicated to the Assyrian goddess Ishtar in what is now Nimrud, northern Iraq.

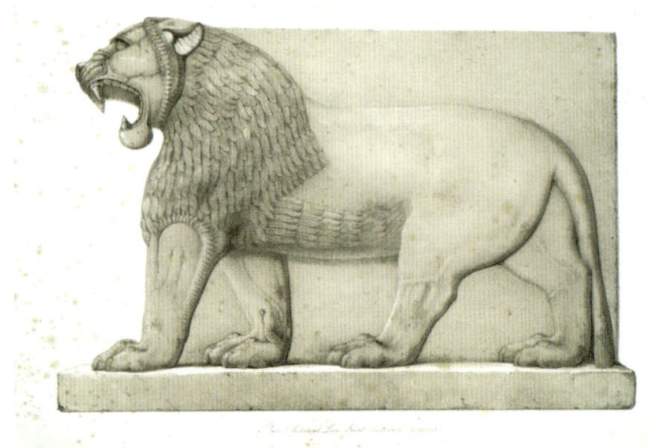

Seated lions by the great French animalier Antoine-Louis Barye (1795–1875) flank the entrance to the Louvre called the Porte des Lions. Barye created the first lion in 1847. Twenty years later it was placed on this site together with a specially cast mirror-image twin.

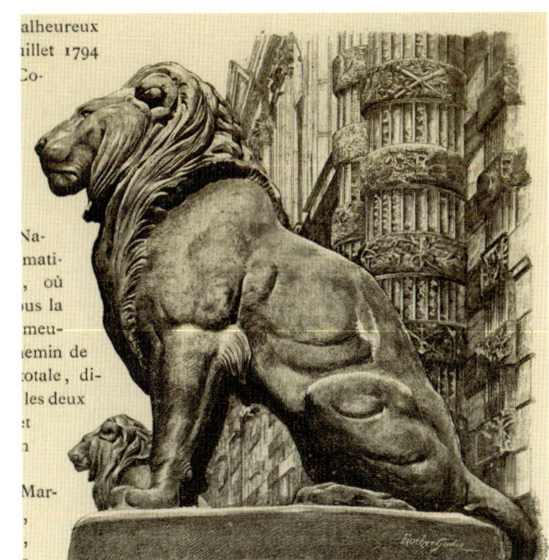

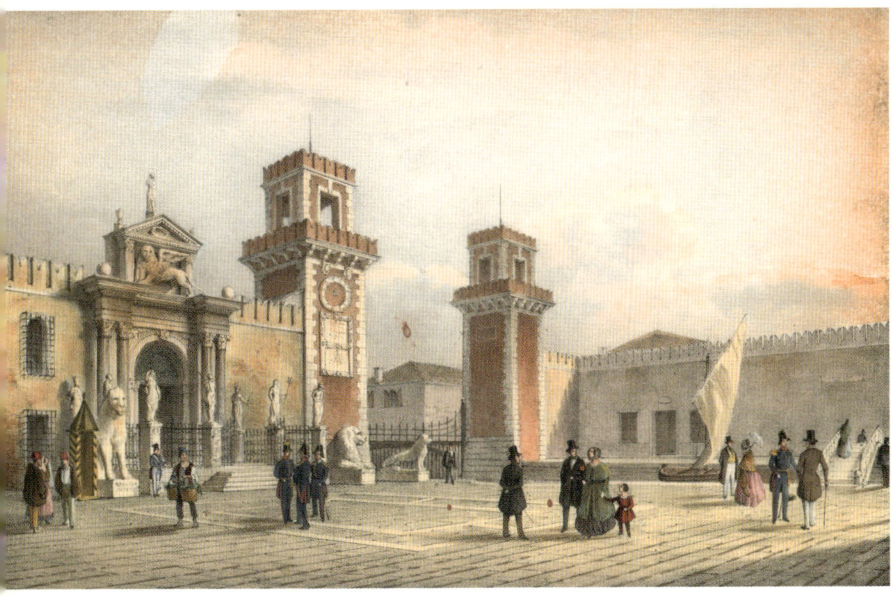

Marco Moro, *L'Arsenal.* Hand-colored lithograph, ca. 1850s. The emblem of Venice, the winged Lion of St. Mark, crowns the main gate of the Arsenal. The two monumental lions flanking the portal were added in 1687.

pair that flanked the steps leading into the gardens of the Villa Medici. Projecting human feelings onto animals, artists have used the big cats to express profound emotion. The Italian neoclassical sculptor Antonio Canova designed a pair of mournful lions to guard the tomb of Pope Clement XIII in St. Peter's Basilica in Rome.

During the American Renaissance (ca. 1880–ca. 1920), of which The New York Public Library's flagship building is a splendid product, architects linked their imposing new buildings with the rich legacy of Europe. In their plan dated 1897, the Library's architects, John Carrère and Thomas Hastings, designated sculptures for four locations on the building's Fifth Avenue façade. The most visible were a pair of lions flanking the entrance stairs off the avenue. In specifying lions for that spot, Carrère and Hastings connected the Library with a long cultural tradition. Their choice was a popular one. The World's Columbian Exposition, held in Chicago in 1893, featured at least eight pairs of lions at the entrances to elaborate Beaux-Arts fair buildings, as well as a Lion Fountain. The following year, a pair of bronze lions by sculptor Edward Kemeys was installed at the entrance to the Art Institute of Chicago, where they have played a role comparable to that of New York City's Library Lions.

At first, a few people complained that The New York Public Library should have chosen an American animal instead of the African lion. One faction proposed a pair of industrious beavers; others suggested elk or moose. Former president Theodore Roosevelt insisted that the bison would

The bronze lion mask that ornaments the drinking fountain of the Second Floor Gallery is just one example of the cornucopia of decorative detail—drawing on motifs from the classical tradition, the natural world, and the animal world—with which Carrère & Hastings lavished both the exterior and the interior of the Library. The architects continued the leonine theme even to the handsome wastepaper basket that they designed for the Library, embellishing it with a lion mask gripping a ring in its mouth on the side and lion paws for feet. More lions are to be found on the building's façade. The first-floor window keystones, which were modeled by Alexander Phimister Proctor, also feature lion masks with rings.

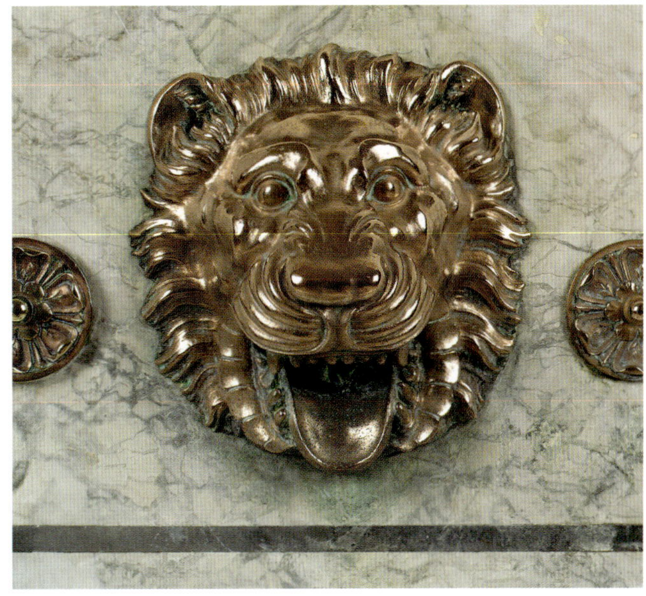

have been most appropriate, arguing that its "shaggy frontlet and mane and short curved horns" were as adaptable to sculpture as the lion's mane while possessing "the advantage of being our own." A generation earlier, Roosevelt's argument might have held sway, but by the 1880s the nationalism represented by the Hudson River School of painters, who celebrated the American wilderness, had been usurped by the cosmopolitan taste of European-trained artists and newly rich collectors who emulated the grandeur of Old World aristocrats. Catering to that taste, Carrère and Hastings insisted on the time-honored lions. Probably on the recommendation of the great American sculptor Augustus Saint-Gaudens, the architects commissioned Edward Clark Potter to execute the sculptures.

Edward Clark Potter

(1857–1923)

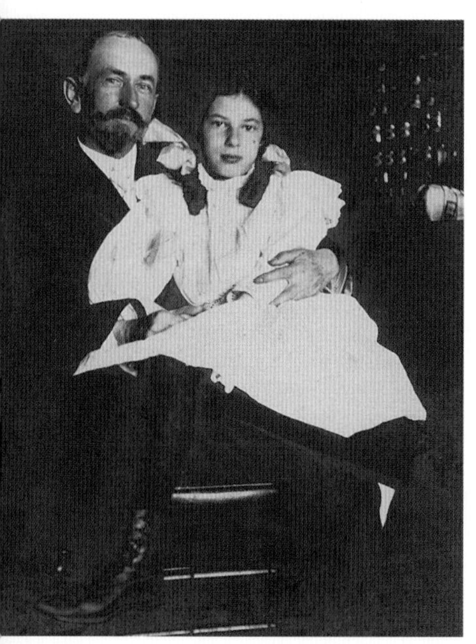

Edward Clark Potter holding one of his two daughters in his lap.

When Edward Clark Potter was commissioned to sculpt the lions flanking the steps of The New York Public Library, he enjoyed the respect of his peers but then, as now, was little known to the public. His aversion to publicity may have been a factor in his obscurity. Henry Wysham Lanier, who in 1906 published an appreciative article on the sculptor, described him as an "extremely modest . . . rather bluff and hearty man . . . free from the . . . slightest pose or self-consciousness."

Potter was born in New London, Connecticut, on November 26, 1857. After three semesters at Amherst College, he left to study at the School of the Museum of Fine Arts in Boston. In 1883 he went to work as studio assistant to Daniel Chester French (1850–1931), who would become a lifelong friend. Potter moved to Vermont in 1885, working as assistant foreman at Proctor's marble quarries and supervising the cutting of sculptures by French. On the older artist's advice, he left in 1887 for Paris, where he studied the human figure under Antonin Mercié, joined Emmanuel Frémiet's classes in animal sculpture at the Paris zoo, and exhibited in the Salons of 1887 and 1888. He returned to the United States in 1889 and exhibited for the first time that year at the National Academy of Design in New York. On New Year's Eve 1890, he married May Dumont, to whom he had been introduced by Mrs. French.

The World's Columbian Exposition in Chicago in 1893 marked a shift in the relationship between French and Potter. No longer mentor and protégé, they became collaborators on a succession of sculptures, with French creating the human figures and Potter the animals. Although journalists routinely gave French the entire credit for these works, he insisted that Potter deserved greater recognition, explaining that neither sculptor confined himself to his part of the composition; both constantly "swapped work and ideas." For the Chicago fair, Potter and French collaborated on the quadriga atop the triumphal arch, as well as on four groups of animals with human attendants installed around the lagoon of the Court of Honor, which were among the most visible and admired of the works created for the Exposition. After the fair, Potter and French worked together on five equestrian monuments, including one of George Washington for Paris. Potter also fulfilled independent commissions for portraits, allegorical figures, and equestrian sculptures, including works for the Gettysburg battlefield, Arlington National Cemetery, the Library of Congress, the Michigan Capitol, and the Brooklyn Museum. His last major work was the first American statue of an aviator, the monument to Colonel Raynal C. Bolling in Greenwich, Connecticut.

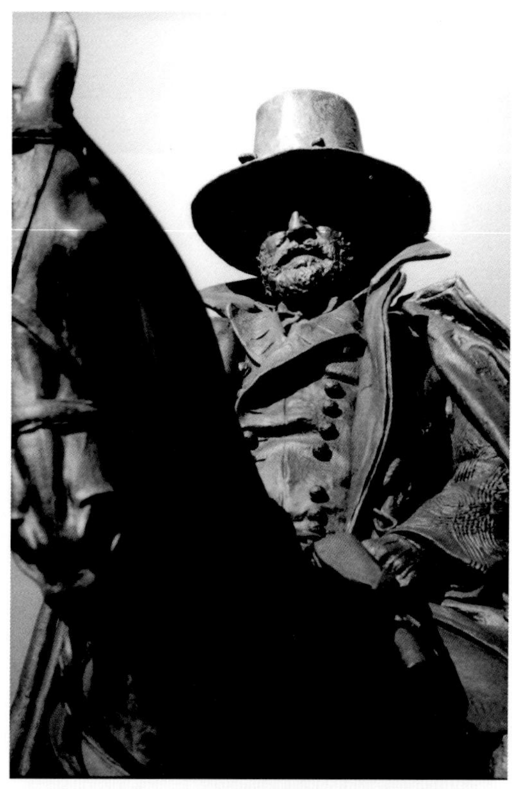

Close-up, Daniel Chester French and Edward Clark Potter, *General Ulysses S. Grant* (see page 19).

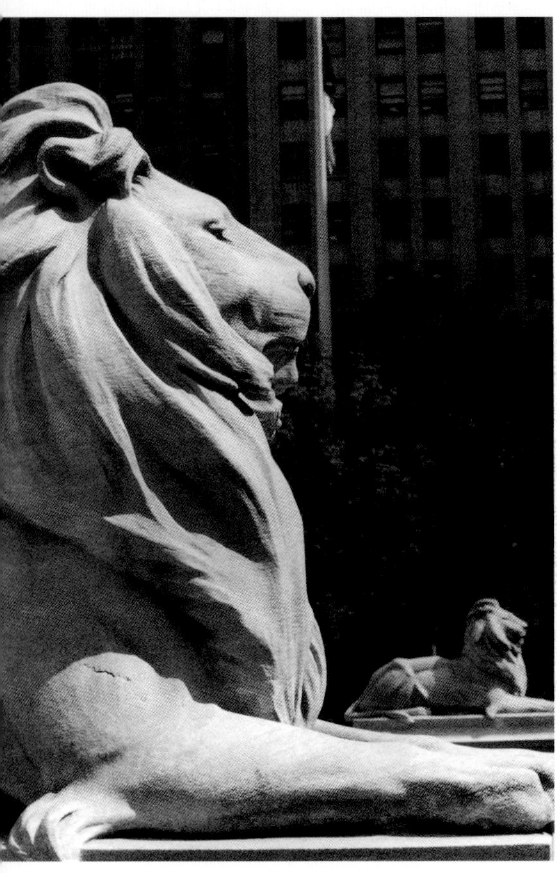

The Library Lions in profile, viewed from the south, 1990.

Potter's achievement as an animalier can be seen not only in the anatomical accuracy of his sculptures but also in his ability to capture the character of his subjects. With equestrian monuments, this meant matching the mood of the horse to that of the rider. In the George Washington sculpture in Paris, the triumphant general sits astride a stately mount; by contrast, in Philadelphia's Fairmount Park, a somber Ulysses S. Grant reins in a handsome steed whose obedience suggests his rider's ability to command the Union troops.

Although he was best known for horses, Potter also sculpted other animals, most notably lions. In the tradition of the French master Antoine-Louis Barye (1796–1875), he produced a few tabletop sculptures of lions devouring their prey. For the gateposts of railroad magnate Collis P. Huntington's four-story brownstone on Fifth Avenue at 57th Street in New York, Potter sculpted a pair of majestic seated lions. In 1903, commissioned to design another pair for the entrance to the Morgan Library on 36th Street between Madison and Park avenues, he departed from tradition, depicting not the usual lions but instead lionesses. The flattened ears, wary vigilance, and tense posture of the Morgan cats suggest potentially dangerous coiled energy. Like the spirited horses restrained by expert riders in Potter's equestrian monuments, these animals convey the power of the man with whom they are associated.

At his home in Greenwich, Connecticut, Potter kept a menagerie that included horses, dogs, cats, sheep, cows,

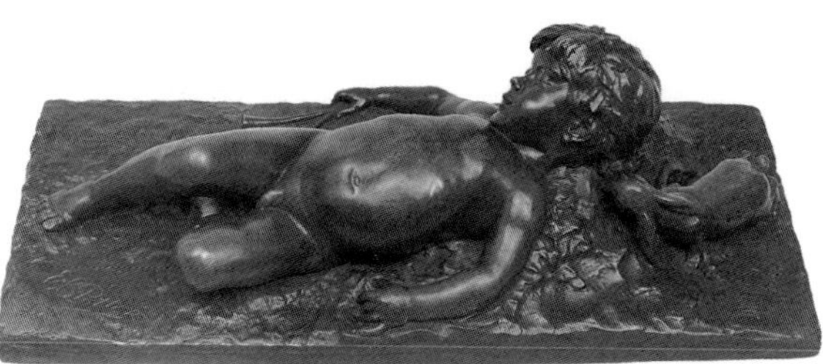

Edward Clark Potter, *Sleeping Faun.*
Bronze, 1887–89; this cast 1919.
The Metropolitan Museum of Art.

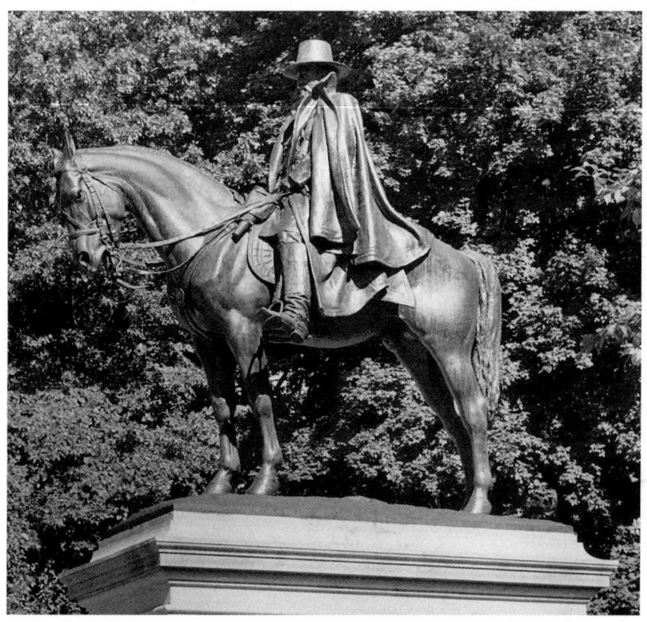

French and Potter,
***General Ulysses S. Grant.* Bronze, 1897.**
Fairmount Park, Philadelphia.

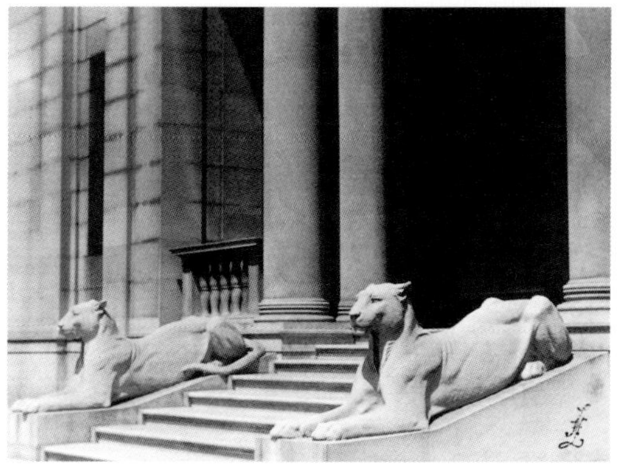

Original entrance to the Morgan Library,
New York, flanked by a pair of marble lionesses
sculpted by Potter ca. 1903.

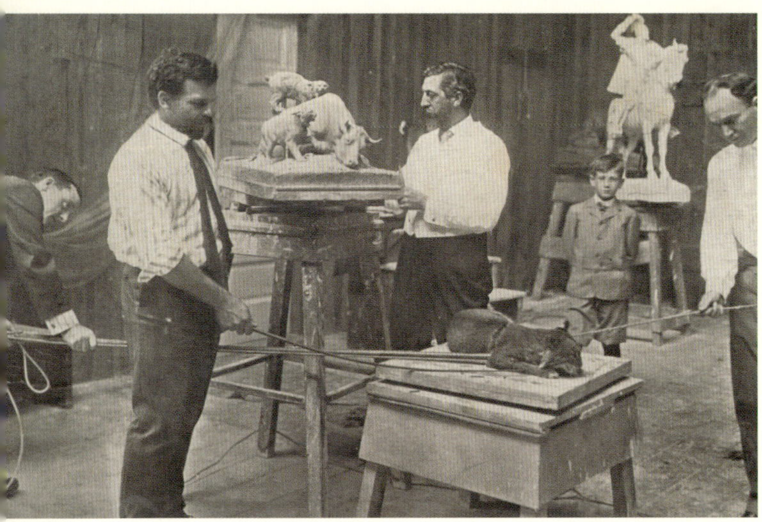

Edward Clark Potter models a live wildcat in his studio in Greenwich, Connecticut, ca. 1903. Assistants restrain the animal while the sculptor's young son Nathan watches.

poultry, rabbits, and occasionally wild animals, all of which he used as models. A photograph taken about 1903 shows Potter at work on a dramatic piece depicting a long-horned steer attacked by two wildcats. He explained to a reporter that he intended "to show that courage, not strength, was the ruling feature in animal life . . . for the wildcats are so small in comparison to the great bulk of the steer that the marvel of it is that the cats could kill it." While the pipe-smoking artist sculpts the clay model and his small son Nathan looks on, assistants restrain a snarling lynx, which Potter kept at his studio for a few weeks. When he was working on the Morgan lionesses, rumors flew that the sculptor would again bring a live model to Greenwich, but Potter reassured a reporter that he would seek his inspiration at the Bronx Zoo.

Potter suffered from nephritis and died in New London on June 21, 1923. The 1930 edition of Lorado Taft's *History of American Sculpture* memorialized him as "a man who knew the horse, head, hock, and barrel, who understood the cat tribe from A to Z, who was at home also in modeling the human form—but who nevertheless, largely because of pert, reiterated journalistic jibes about his fine 'Lions' in front of The New York Public Library, failed to receive all the honor due him."

French and Potter, *Indian Corn* or *Plenty,* 1893. This was one of four monumental human and animal pairs the sculptors created to surround the Lagoon of the Court of Honor at the World's Columbian Exposition, Chicago. Like most of the sculpture commissioned for the Fair, it was made of staff, an impermanent mixture of plaster and fiber.

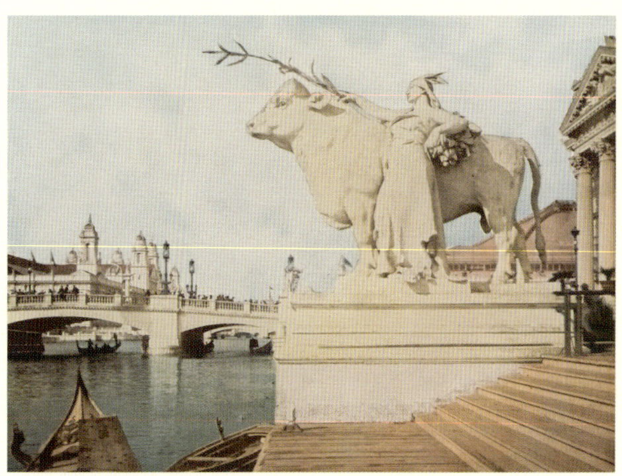

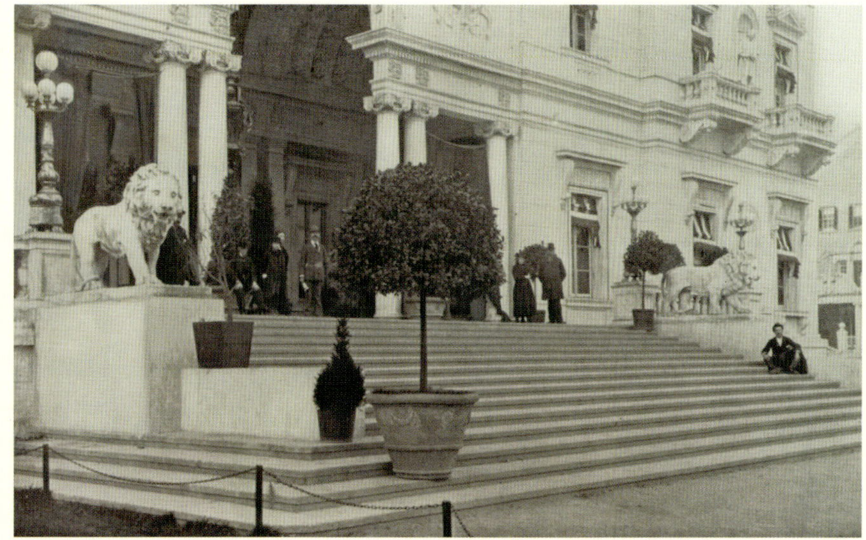

The New York State Building at the World's Columbian Exposition, with a pair of lions by Potter flanking the entrance staircase.

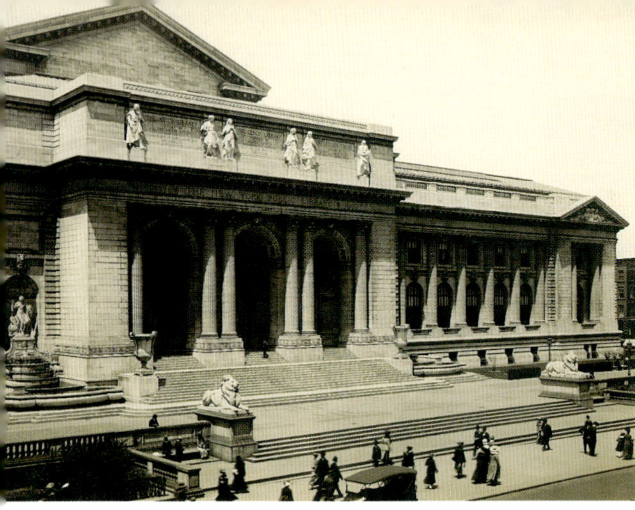

A view of the recently completed Library, ca. 1915, by the Wurts Brothers, the esteemed firm of architectural photographers that was based in New York from the 1890s through the 1970s.

Potter was an excellent choice. One of America's most distinguished animaliers, he had already designed numerous lions. For the New York State Building at the World's Columbian Exposition, Potter gave three-dimensional form to a Renaissance bas-relief of a striding lion on the staircase of the Palazzo Barberini in Rome. He also sculpted the fearsome lionesses installed at the entrance to the Morgan Library on Madison Avenue at 36th Street in 1903. Potter received $10,000 for the Morgan sculptures. Seven years later, he was paid only $8,000 for the larger lions at The New York Public Library. The art budget for the new Library had been slashed, however, and artists accepted low fees out of civic duty.

The architects established the pose, showing reclining lions in their drawings of the Library's Fifth Avenue façade. Either Potter or the architects changed the sculptures' position, however. In Carrère and Hastings' original plan, the cats faced one another, overlooking pedestrians climbing the steps to the building's entrance but ignoring the street. Turned to face Fifth Avenue, they became guardians not only of the Library and its patrons, but also of all passersby.

Potter sketched the lions at the Bronx Zoo before producing realistic small-scale models. When Hastings inspected the maquettes, as Potter's friend Henry Wysham Lanier told newspaper columnist N. S. Olds forty years later, he "praised the life-likeness of the big cats, but finally said he felt they should be somewhat more 'architectural.'" Potter struggled with revisions, "changing posture, facial expressions and so on, trying to match some admittedly vague idea in the architect's mind. The final result was not as real or powerful as the first clay sketch, but while it did not satisfy Potter's artist eye, it was accepted, and he went ahead on that basis."

Working with assistants at his studio in Greenwich, Connecticut, Potter prepared a full-sized model in clay of only one lion, the southerly one. A photograph of the large model accompanied the application to the Municipal Art Commission, which gave its preliminary approval on April 12, 1910. Artisans then reversed the pose, creating plaster casts of the leonine twins. In late September, the plaster models were installed on their pedestals on the Fifth Avenue plaza so that their relationship to the site could be evaluated before the lions were carved in marble.

Almost immediately, the mockery began. The sculptures were not judged by knowledgeable art critics, but rather they were ridiculed by general reporters. They were called "absurd," "squash-faced," "mealy-mouthed, complacent creatures." One writer derided their supposed resemblance to Norwegian dramatist Henrik Ibsen. *The New York Times* published a "defense" of the sculptures on September 28, 1910, that was merely a vehicle for the writer's witticisms. "As plaster lions go, these are of far above average merit," the editorial began. It continued:

Sculpting a Marble Monument

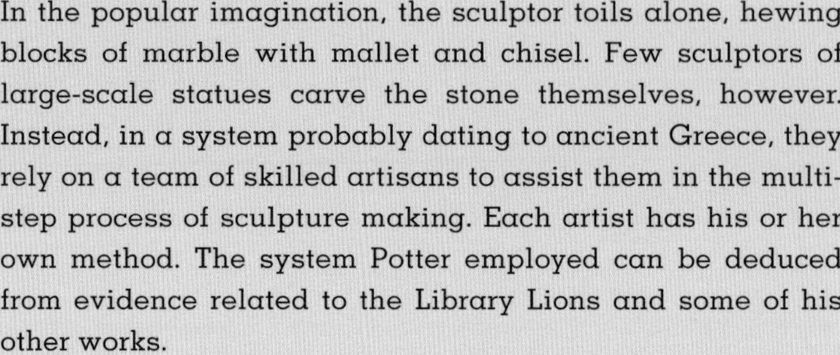

In the popular imagination, the sculptor toils alone, hewing blocks of marble with mallet and chisel. Few sculptors of large-scale statues carve the stone themselves, however. Instead, in a system probably dating to ancient Greece, they rely on a team of skilled artisans to assist them in the multi-step process of sculpture making. Each artist has his or her own method. The system Potter employed can be deduced from evidence related to the Library Lions and some of his other works.

Potter's pencil sketches for an equestrian monument reveal him working out his first thoughts on paper. Next, he developed his ideas in small wax or clay models, experimenting with several versions before selecting one to carry to completion. (For the Library, he in fact designed only one lion; later in the process, artisans reversed the pose to create the second.) After the Library's architects approved the small version of the lion, the sculptor had his assistants build an armature to support a full-sized, highly finished clay model. The studio assistants also prepared the clay, moistening a fresh batch every morning, spraying it occasionally to keep it malleable, and covering it at the end of each day to prevent it from drying prematurely. Potter used three tons of clay to model the Morgan Library lioness; the larger NYPL lion would have demanded much more. As he worked by hand and tool, Potter paid special attention to the play of light and shadow over the surfaces, occasionally rolling the huge model out of his studio to evaluate it in natural light, sensitive to its changes in appearance at different times of day.

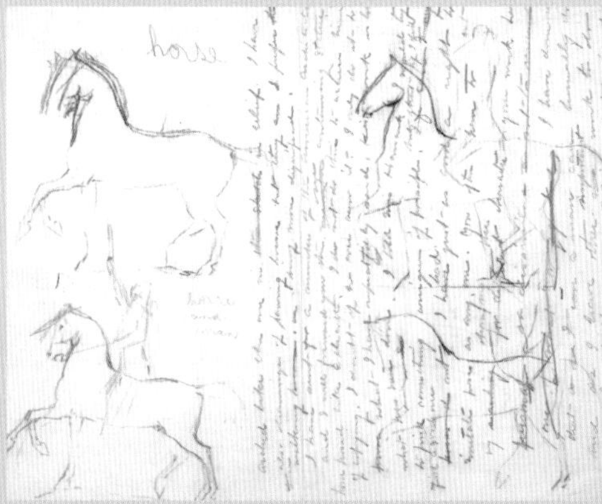

Edward Clark Potter, undated draft of a letter to a client. He wrote on the reverse, "I will send you this evening several photographs of my sketches," apparently referring to more-finished versions of his pencil drawings of horses both recto and verso. Additional pencil notes in a juvenile hand or hands were probably made by one or more of his three children.

Because clay is fragile, the sculptor's assistants then produced a plaster mold of the finished large model. Next, using the plaster mold, they made a full-sized plaster cast. To make the second lion, either Potter's assistants or specialists from the Piccirilli brothers' stone-carving studio used a precise system of reversing the measurements from an established center point to make a mirror image of the first lion. The plaster casts embodied the sculptor's design but lacked both the immediacy of the original clay and the rich gleam of the finished marble. As the Italian neo-classical sculptor Antonio Canova observed, "Sculpture is born in clay, dies in plaster, and is resurrected in marble." The dull finish of the plaster models may have contributed to the unexpected criticism when they were set on the granite pedestals in front of the Library for final evaluation by Potter and the architects.

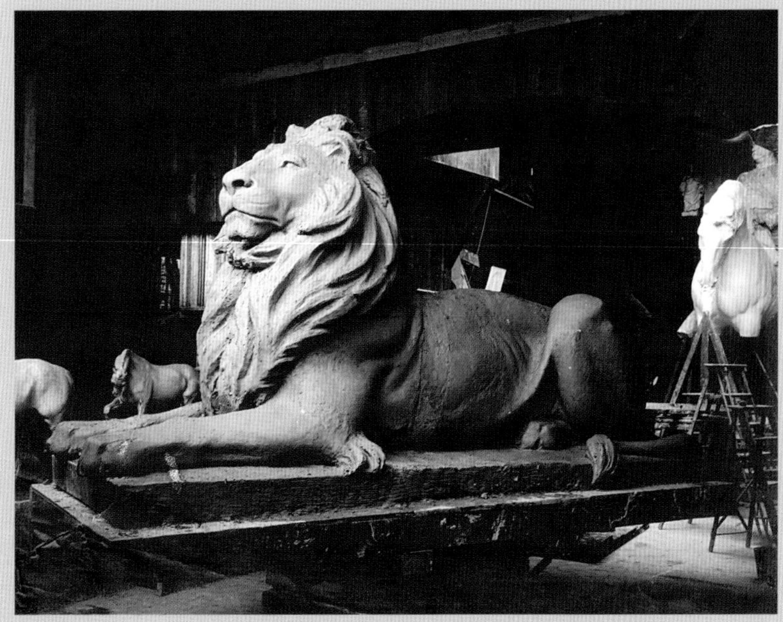

Full-size clay model of the southerly Lion in Potter's Greenwich studio, surrounded by other works in progress.

Once the Municipal Art Commission approved the full-sized models, the plasters were shipped to the Piccirillis' studio in the Bronx. There, artisans transferred the exact measurements of the plaster casts to enormous blocks of Tennessee pink marble. They began by measuring the sculptures' outside

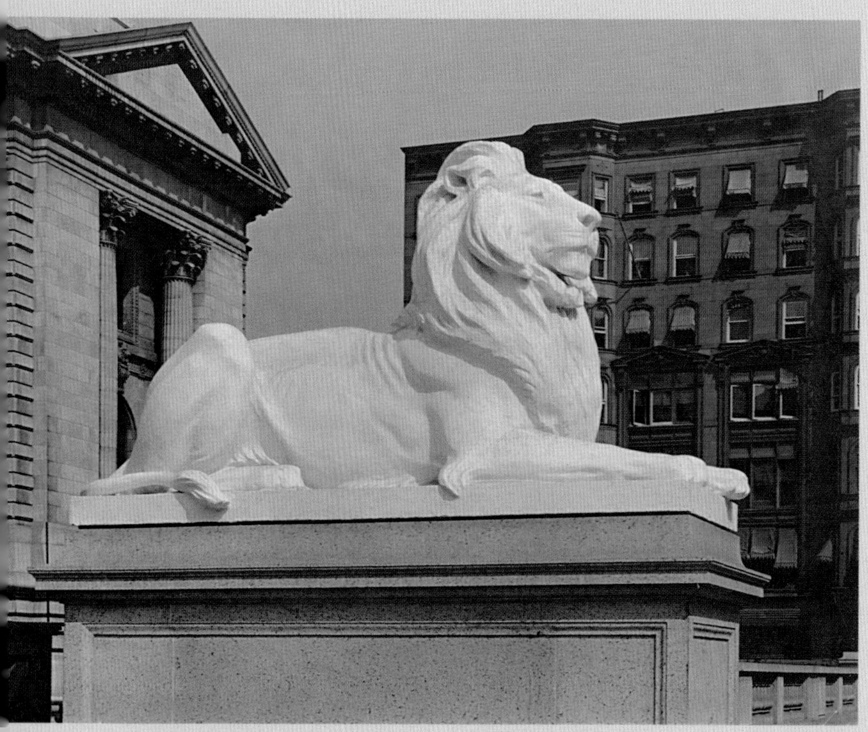

Full-scale plaster model of the northerly Lion on its pedestal in front of The New York Public Library, late September 1910.

dimensions: the top of the mane, the farthest points of the forepaws and tail, and the widest expanse of the haunches. Those measurements were transferred to the blocks and the approximate shapes roughed out. Next, a mechanical device called a pointing machine was used to measure the depth from one plane to another (for example, from the eyelid to the cheek). The machine then drilled a hole to the desired depth, leaving a metal point to mark the spot. When the marble bristled with points, artisans cut away the excess stone. The work became progressively more detailed, with senior artisans taking over from less experienced ones as the desired forms emerged. Step by step, the team carved the marble blocks until they matched the plaster casts. At the end of the process, Potter probably made small refinements to the finished sculptures before they were installed in front of the Library.

> *They do not suggest nearly as much as does the lion of St. Mark's the results a biologist would expect to get from crossing a dachshund with a Welsh rabbit, and if they do not look as much like real lions as does the lion of Lucerne or the one in the Bargello of Venice, that is nothing against them. . . . [They] differ in many respects from those that wander over African plains. . . . As library lions, however, they are all right. Their cast of countenance is distinctly reflective and intellectual, and if their faces show a combination of melancholy and ennui, that is natural enough in the circumstances.*

That writer was at least amusing, but most of the criticism was as clumsy as it was uninformed. A typical example was a letter to the *Times* of September 30, 1910, in which the writer, identified only as E.C.B., attacked the anatomical knowledge of the experienced animalier: "Anyone with a child's knowledge of animals must need stand in open-eyed wonder before these monstrosities. The head is possibly a lion's. The body resembles what might be a cross between a hippopotamus and a cow; as for those semi-human hind legs, words fail."

Why did Potter's lions arouse such virulent criticism? They do not deserve it on artistic grounds, for they admirably suit the site. Their complacence, derided by many, is characteristic of male lions, which spend much of their time sleeping, while it is the more active females that do most of the

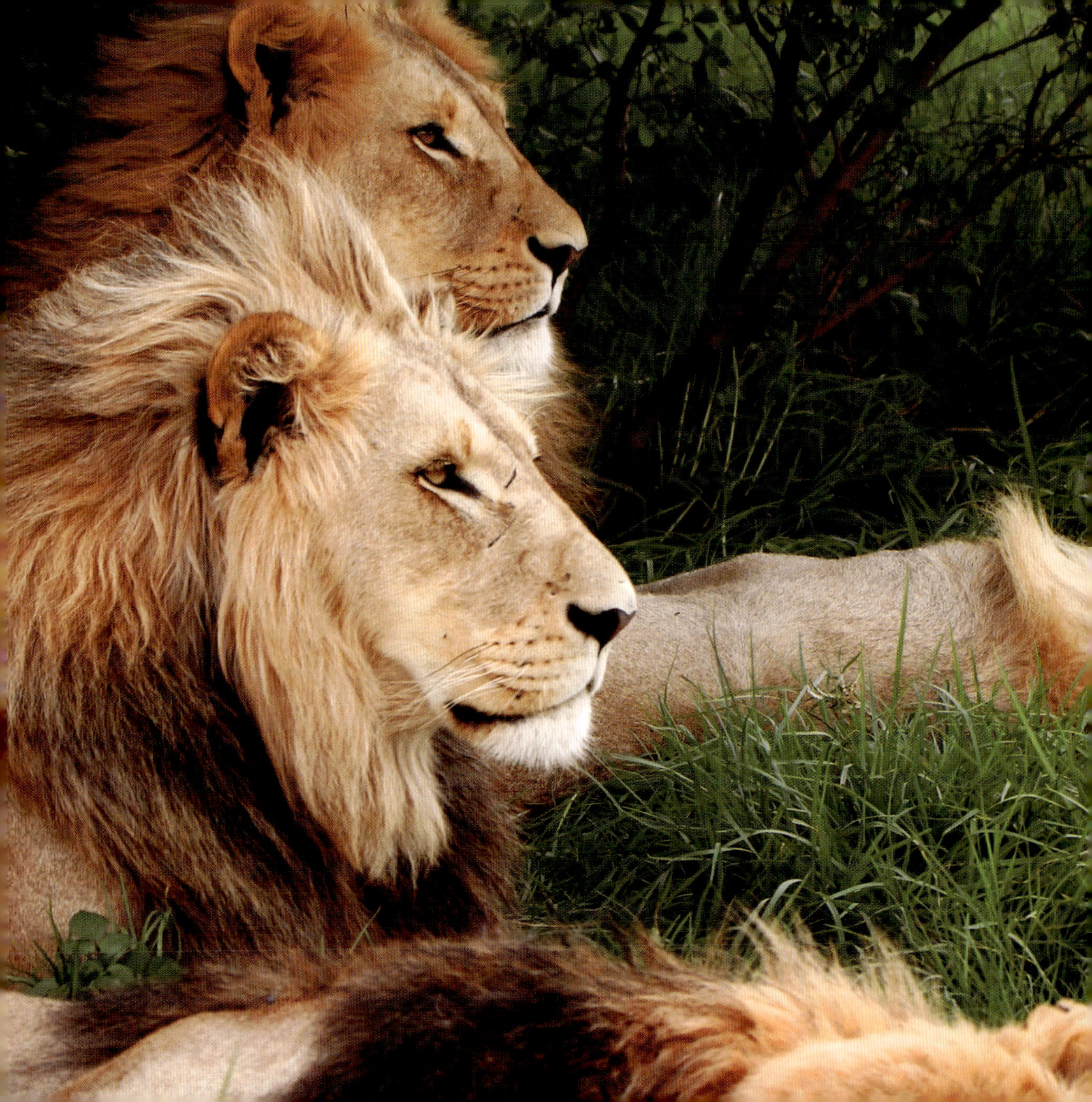

Lions in the Wild

THE LIBRARY LIONS ARE LARGER THAN LIFE, EACH STRETCHING MORE THAN eleven feet (not counting the tail), about three feet longer than their wild prototypes. Exaggerated scale is typical of outdoor sculptures, which must be over-life-sized to appear natural. In other respects, however, artist Edward Clark Potter was faithful to the appearance of the King of the Beasts. The sculpted lions' raised heads signal dominance and, although they are reclining, their tensed muscles indicate alertness.

The largest predator in Africa, lions occupy grassy plains, savannas, and open woodlands. Distinguished from other cats by their sociability, they live in prides, extended families comprising about a dozen adult females, one to six adult males, and numerous cubs. The pride dozes together during the day, the cubs tumbling among them, lazily chasing the distinctive black tuft at the end of the adults' long tails. Toward dusk, yawning profusely, the animals awaken. They engage in mutual grooming and head rubbing until, roaring in chorus, small groups head out in search of water and prey. This cooperative behavior extends to the rearing of the young. After a gestation period of three and a half months, a lioness delivers a litter of two, three, or occasionally four cubs. She hides the newborns, each weighing only two to four pounds, for about a month, until they are able to follow her from thicket or crevice to meet the rest of the pride. There, because the females breed all at the same time, the youngsters will join other cubs of about the same age and will be allowed to suckle from any lactating female.

Young males leave their birth pride when they are about three years old, roaming and hunting together for a year or two until they take over a group of females, driving out the older males. The newly dominant lions protect the pride from intruding bachelors. They leave most of the hunting to the females, muscling in after the kill to claim "the lion's share." Then it's back to sleep—the big cats spend about 80 percent of their time at rest.

Lions at rest in a game preserve in South Africa.

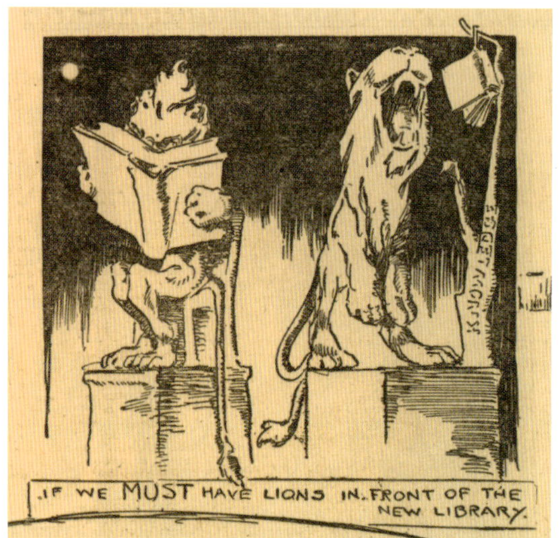

This cartoon, the first known to feature the lions, appeared in *The New York Times* on October 16, 1910, part of a full-page gallery by Hy. Mayer of his "Impressions of the Passing Show."

hunting. Indeed, the Library Lions embody the aristocratic dignity conventionally associated with guardian lions.

One likely explanation for the criticism is that the Library's most conspicuous ornaments became scapegoats for the institution itself. From the beginning, the construction of the Library was plagued by political controversy and labor disputes. When Carrère and Hastings signed the contract in December 1897, the work was expected to be completed in three years. Instead, it dragged on for fourteen. After years of enduring the unsightly, disruptive construction on the city's main thoroughfare, New Yorkers were exasperated. Ironically, then, the Lions' role as symbols of the Library began in animosity.

However petty its origins, the controversy embarrassed an institution weary of confrontation. The beleaguered architects were so eager to end it that they made the public, to a degree, collaborators in the art that they had commissioned. In response to complaints that the lions were too hairy, they had Potter shave their manes. A comparison of the photograph of the model of the southerly lion in Potter's studio with one taken several months later reveals that the once-luxuriant mane had been slicked down, a slight part reducing its bulk. Hastings promised further changes. When passersby protested that the plaster lions were too large, he reassured a *Times* reporter that the marble figures would be scaled down. Fortunately, this change was made subtly, if at all.

The architects' application for final approval of the sculptures "urgently" requested quick action. The Municipal Art Commission granted its approval on October 11, 1910. Five days later, the lions made what was probably their first cartoon appearance. The drawing in the Sunday *New York Times* shows two scrawny beasts reading atop pedestals shaped like books. Although the caption ("If we *must* have lions in front of the new library") implies that it would be better not to have the sculptures at all, the cartoon conveys an amused affection that would only grow with time.

While Potter endured the taunts of the press, two enormous blocks of Tennessee pink marble were shipped to New York City. A favorite of sculptors because of its density and resistance to weathering, this marble looks pink only when polished; otherwise, it appears almost white. Carrère and Hastings reported to Library director John S. Billings on September 30, 1910, that the blocks chosen for the lion sculptures, each measuring approximately twelve feet long by six feet high and twelve feet wide, were the largest ever taken from the Tennessee quarries, adding that "each stone took sixteen horses to move from yard to yard." The task of converting Potter's full-sized plaster models into marble fell to the Piccirilli brothers, America's leading stone carvers. The Piccirillis received $5,000 for their work, which involved

The Piccirilli Brothers

Many nineteenth-century American sculptors lived in Italy to enjoy access not only to marble quarries but also to artisans able to transform a small model into an over-life-sized monument. Shipping large sculptures across the Atlantic was expensive, however, and as the demand for public monuments grew, quarries opened in Vermont, Tennessee, and other states. Just as important was the emergence of a group of highly skilled artisans, many of them immigrants, capable of realizing the conceptions of master sculptors. The best known of those workshops was that of the Piccirilli brothers in New York.

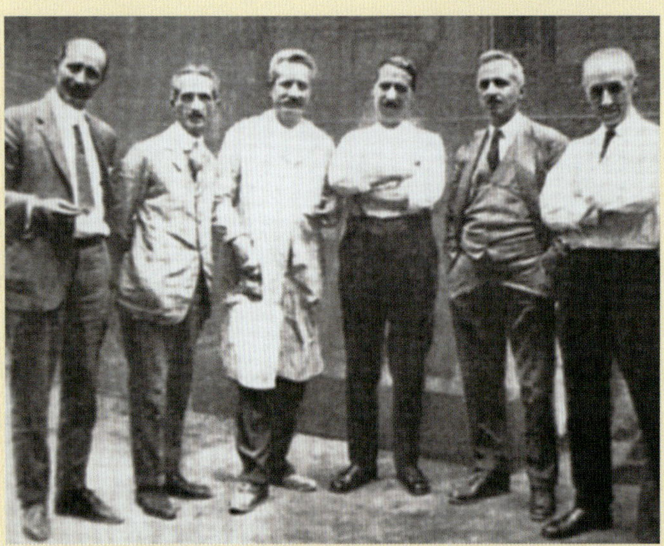

The Piccirilli brothers, ca. 1930.
Left to right: Getulio, Furio, Attilio, Ferruccio, Masaniello, and Orazio.

The Piccirilli (pronounced peach-er-EEL-y) family hailed from Massa, Italy, at the center of the famous Carrara marble quarries, where the father, Giuseppe, had a stone-carving atelier. He taught all six of his sons the rudiments of sculpture; two of them, Attilio and Furio, studied at the prestigious Accademia di San Luca in Rome, where their father had trained. In 1888 the family emigrated to the United States, settling in New York. By 1890, they had opened their first studio in a rented stable on Sixth Avenue at 39th Street in Manhattan. Two years later they moved to the Bronx, purchased property at 467 East 142nd Street, and constructed three interconnecting three-story brick buildings and a one-story annex around a courtyard. At the time, it was the largest studio in the United States. The complex encompassed elegantly furnished living quarters, individual studios for each of the brothers, immense spaces for creating monumental sculpture, exhibition rooms, and apartments that were sometimes used by visiting sculptors.

Each brother brought special gifts to the family enterprise. Attilio excelled in the human form, Furio in animals and bas-relief, Orazio in animals and ornament, and Ferruccio and Masaniello in ornamental sculpture. Getulio, also a master carver, served as business manager. In addition to executing the designs of other artists, some of the Piccirillis became known as sculptors in their own right. Attilio, the most successful, is best remembered for the Maine Monument at the southwest corner of Central Park in New York City. Not limited to stonework, he also produced an innovative glass relief for Manhattan's Rockefeller Center.

A skilled staff assisted the brothers in the execution of such famous monuments as Daniel Chester French's seated Lincoln in the Lincoln Memorial in Washington, DC, as well as architectural sculpture, including the pediment of the United States Supreme Court Building. For The New York Public Library, the Piccirilli brothers carved not only the Lions but also, high up on the Fifth Avenue façade, Paul Wayland Bartlett's allegorical figures representing History, Romance, Religion, Poetry, Drama, and Philosophy. Jerry Capa, who as a young sculpture student was a regular visitor to the Piccirilli compound, counted one hundred coat hooks lining the entrance hallway—an indication of the staff size sometimes needed to fulfill the brothers' commissions. Among their employees who carved the Library Lions were August Beretta, Salvatore Mutoli, and Joseph Mutoli.

The full-scale plaster model of the southerly Lion on a dolly in the Piccirilli brothers' yard in the Bronx. The stonework above the doorway exemplifies the embellishments that graced the studio compound. "You came in from the streets of New York and entered the Renaissance," Jerry Capa recalled.

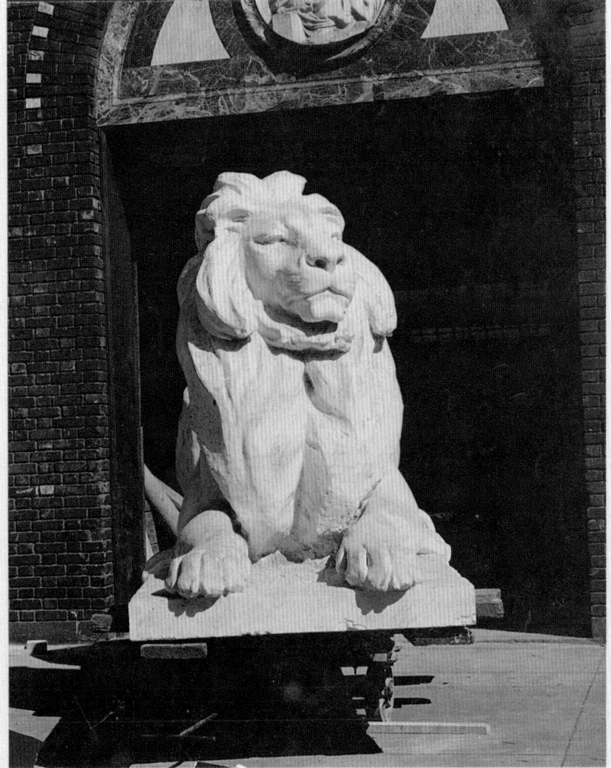

The Bronx establishment exuded an Old World atmosphere. Critic Lorado Taft compared it to "a Florentine household of the Quattrocento." At noon every Saturday, the workweek ended with lunch served family style on a long refectory table. Adeline Adams, whose husband, Herbert, commissioned the Piccirillis to carve his marble sculptures, described feasts of homemade pasta, roasted meats, Italian cheese and sausage, fresh vegetables, "and the good Vesuvian grape always in seemly circulation!" Conversation (in English, French, and Italian) sparkled—not surprisingly, since the guests might include mayor Fiorello La Guardia, tenor Enrico Caruso, other civic and cultural leaders (presidents Theodore Roosevelt, William Howard Taft, and Woodrow Wilson all visited), and, of course, some of America's leading sculptors.

Two of the brothers returned to Italy in the 1920s, but the workshop thrived into the 1930s. Attilio died in his studio in October 1945, just three days after the death of Getulio. The business was closed in 1946, and the buildings were demolished some years later. Through the hard work of local residents and educators Mary Shelley and Bill Carroll, East 142nd Street between Brook and Willis avenues was renamed Piccirilli Place in 2004.

CARRÈRE AND HASTINGS, ARCHITECTS
225 Fifth Avenue
New York

JOHN M CARRÈRE, F.A.I.A.
THOMAS HASTINGS, F.A.I.A.
OWEN BRAINARD, C.E.

September 30, 1910.

Dear Doctor Billings:

Our superintendent at the Library, Mr. Woolston, stated in his daily report just received, that "the two stones for the lions of the Library are at Piccirilli's Yard. Mr. O'Reilly reports that these two pieces of marble are the largest ever taken from the Tennessee quarries and each stone took sixteen horses to move from yard to yard".

The size of these blocks is approximately 12'-0" long, 6'-0" high and 12'-0" wide. We thought that this might be of interest to the Committee when considering the photographs of the lions.

Very truly yours,

Doctor John S. Billings,
425 Lafayette Street,
New York.

Letter from Carrère and Hastings, Architects, to John S. Billings, director of The New York Public Library, announcing the arrival of the marble for the lions at the Piccirillis' yard, September 30, 1910. The architect's superintendent at the Library reports that "these two pieces of marble are the largest ever taken from the Tennessee quarries and each stone took sixteen horses to move from yard to yard."

transferring the exact measurements of the plaster models to the stone by use of a device called a pointing machine and cutting away the excess stone.

The completed lions were set in front of the Library a week before its official opening on May 23, 1911. An unidentified newspaper reporting their installation called the sculptures "noble in mien," with "an air of force and dignity which makes them peculiarly appropriate as ornaments" of the Library, adding that the "figures have been much praised by artists and connoisseurs since put in place." Nonetheless, the media-driven derision clung so tenaciously to the sculptures that when Potter fell and broke a wrist in November 1911, the *Times* report of the accident identified him only as "sculptor of the much-criticised lions of the New York Public Library." Further taunts surfaced five years later where Potter must least have expected them, in *American Art News*. S. H. P. Pell of New York City wrote to the editor in 1916, "I have suspected for some time that the model for the good natured lions in front of the public library . . . was a stuffed one. On careful examination I am confirmed in my opinion. Directly behind the right foreleg of the northernmost lion is a patch showing distinctly that whoever executed the copy was more than Chinese in his love for detail and exact reproduction." (The patch to which Pell referred was a repair made at the Piccirilli yard to correct a flaw in the marble.) Daniel Chester French, then America's most esteemed sculptor, hotly rebuked the journal's editors for publishing a letter he called "not only useless and silly, but cruel and unjust." The indignant French wrote, "The statues which are treated so flippantly are the serious product of a sculptor who, as you know, has produced and is producing works of exceptional merit, and who has the high respect of his fellow artists. I think you, too, should accord him the respect which his talents and his sincerity have won for him in the art world."

Potter died in 1923, no doubt still considering the Lions a humiliating failure. In his obituary, few newspapers listed The New York Public Library's Lions among his noteworthy sculptures; one mistakenly grouped them with his equestrian monuments as "the Lyons statue in front of the Public Library, New York." But, even then, the true public attitude toward the Library Lions was emerging, and it was dramatically different from the condescending mockery that had filled so many columns. "These Potter beasts have long passed beyond the realm of dispute as completely as the Victorian lions [by Sir Edwin Landseer] at the base of the Nelson monument in Trafalgar Square in London," a posthumous tribute in an unidentified newspaper preserved in the artist's papers at the Archives of American Art asserted. In a letter to the editor of *The New York Times* published on July 8, 1923, the painter and art critic James Britton wrote, "I no more doubt that the great library sentinels

"How long you been standin' here—I was waitin' in front of the other lion!"

One of Roland Coe's cartoons collected in *Coe's Crosstown Carnival,* published by the Haddon Craftsmen in 1935.

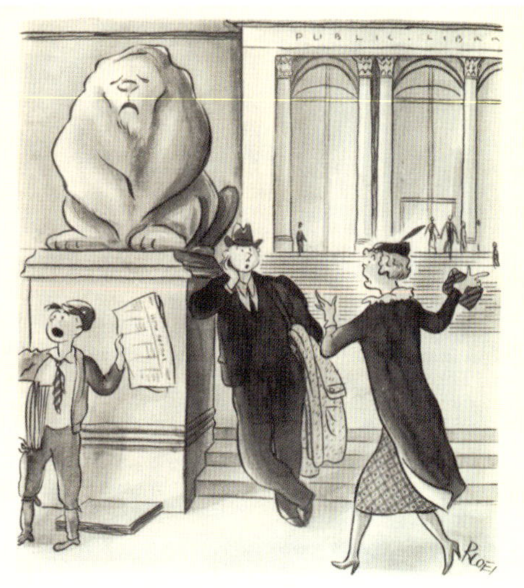

hold close to first place in popularity among the sculptures of America than that these lions artistically surpass in merit anything ornamental in the embellishment of this conspicuous facade." From that time on, the press followed the public, reflecting their attitude in cartoons and reporting the nicknames, seasonal ornamentation, and anecdotes that clearly demonstrated widespread affection for the sculptures. Two themes underlay the varied expressions of this authentic public response: the sculptures' site and their subject.

The Lions' location near one of New York's busiest intersections makes them a reassuring landmark, a convenient rendezvous. They are bold accents in a great urban space, which they enhance without invading. A 1932 *New Yorker* cartoon played on their role as meeting place—scrawled on one Lion's rump is the message, "Mr. Knox, I couldn't wait any longer. Mabel." During World War II, a soldier who couldn't keep a date sent a telegram to his girlfriend addressed simply "Care of the North Lion, Public Library." Roland Coe's amusing cartoon, published in a collection of his work in 1935, is yet another variation on this theme.

The sculptures' subject is also central to their popularity. As animals, and placid ones at that, they inspire a response that today no allegorical figures, obelisks, or portrait sculptures could possibly evoke, even on the same site. They are not subject to the obsolescence of sculptures that embody discarded values or that portray now-forgotten "great men," nor do they evoke the reverence that surrounds such meaning-laden works as the Statue of Liberty. Instead, the Library Lions can carry whatever personal meanings the public wants to project onto them. Cartoonists and storytellers have long imagined them as living creatures, usually with the characteristics of humans or household pets. A 1935 *New Yorker* cartoon by George Price shows a policeman bewildered by a litter of cubs around one pedestal. Another *New Yorker* cartoon, Richard Taylor's "Revised Statuary for the City of Tomorrow," shows scholarly Lions wearing spectacles, heads propped on paws, while they read enormous books.

As highly visible, much-loved landmarks, the Lions have marked the emotional life of the city in good times and bad. During World War I, book drives for soldiers took up position at the feet of the Lions. Starting in 1950, the city's holiday festivities seemed to begin only when the Lions were adorned with giant wreaths. In 2001, red, white, and blue ribbons on the wreaths expressed the city's renewed patriotism after the trauma of 9/11. Other adornments marked happier occasions. For the Subway Series of 2000, the downtown Lion sported a Yankees cap, his uptown brother a Mets topper.

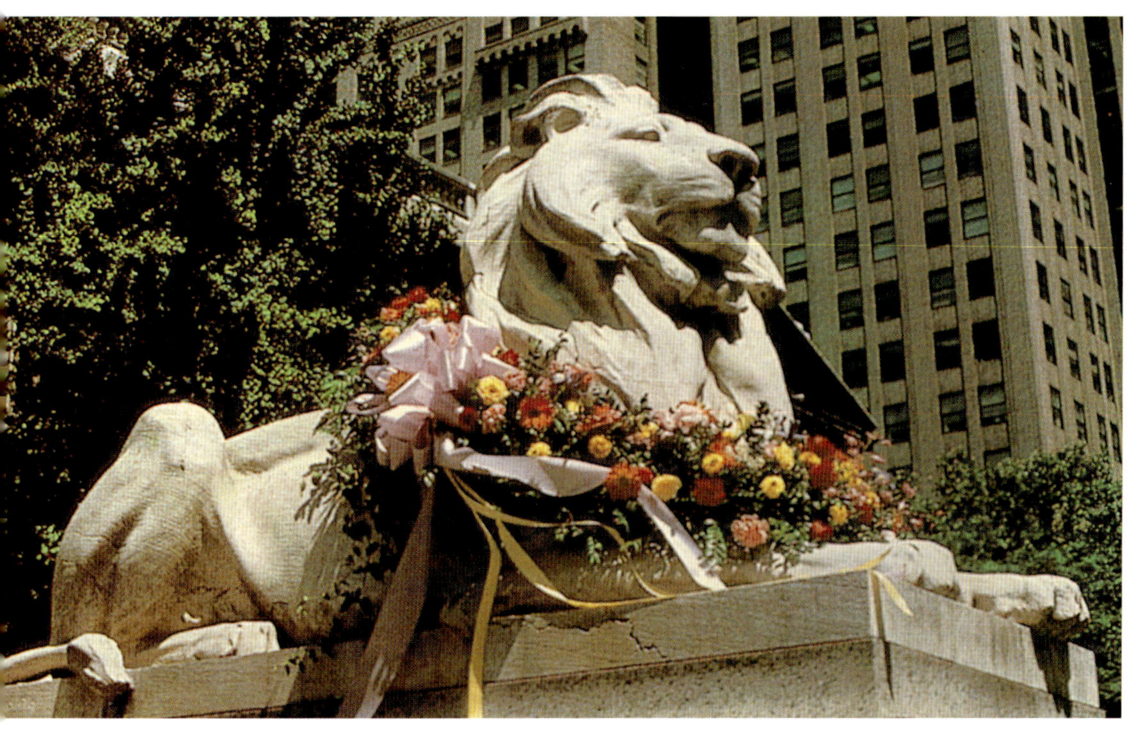

The northerly Lion bedecked with a floral wreath to mark Fragrance Week NYC, 1979.

Playing on the urban legend that the beasts would roar when a virgin passed by, the institution added recorded roars to the Christmas wreaths in 1979. The Lions roared every day at noon to thank the public for year-end contributions to its "feed the lions" campaign. The ploy worked: it was the first year the Library did not operate at a deficit. One of the wreaths was stolen but later returned, and the Lions roared again in 1980. But again one wreath was stolen, so that bit of metropolitan whimsy was sadly abandoned.

What's in a Name?

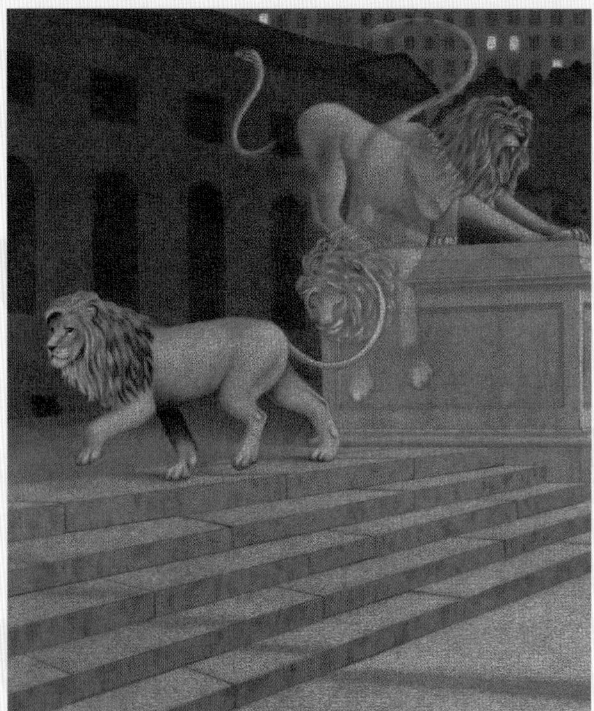

"Rollo had turned golden, too, and was stretching and yawning like a waking housecat. He carefully inched down his pedestal and finally leaped the last few inches to the ground." From *Hilary & the Lions* (1990), by Frank DeSaix and Debbi Durland DeSaix.

The Lions have never had "official" names, appearing in Library documents simply as the northerly Lion and the southerly Lion. But one measure of the public's affection is the nicknames people have given the sculptures over the years. Perhaps the first were Peter Cooper and Horace Greeley, after two prominent nineteenth-century New Yorkers. Cooper was a leading manufacturer and philanthropist; Greeley, an influential abolitionist and newspaperman. But it was the two men's chin whiskers that prompted an editor of *American Art News* to apply their names to the similarly bewhiskered Lions.

The New Yorker, which has featured the Lions in numerous cartoons and covers, once sensibly suggested that they be called simply Uptown and Downtown. Ignoring the Lions' gender, some wits have given them boy-girl names: Leo and Leonora, Pyramus and Thisbe (for the doomed lovers of classical mythology), Lord Lenox and Lady Astor (honoring Library founders James Lenox and John Jacob Astor), and, in a skit staged by the Library staff in 1935, Plato and Lily, proud parents of the cubs Franklin, Eleanor, and Tiny. Anne Carroll Moore, NYPL's first head of Children's Services, celebrated the institution's history while acknowledging the Lions' gender, calling them Leo Lenox and Leo Astor in her children's book, *Nicholas: A Manhattan Christmas Story,* published in 1924. In Moore's story, Leo Lenox, the southerly Lion, keeps an eye on the pedestrians coming down Fifth Avenue, while Leo Astor looks out for those heading uptown. In a later children's book, *Hilary & the Lions* (1990), with story by Frank DeSaix and pictures by Debbi Durland DeSaix, the Lions, now dubbed Ainsley and Rollo, take care of a young girl who gets lost during a visit to the city.

The Lions' best-known nicknames, Patience and Fortitude, are credited to New York mayor Fiorella La Guardia. The mayor used the phrase to sign off his popular Sunday afternoon radio broadcasts, which aired from 1942 to 1945. "The people of this city have two cardinal virtues, Patience and Fortitude," he told a reporter. Whether it was La Guardia himself or someone else who assigned his tagline to the Lions, the nicknames have made them stand for "the people of this city." Occasionally, the names are given an odd twist when people misremember them. A researcher who was annoyed by the scraping of other readers' chairs on the waxed marble floor of the Rose Main Reading Room persuaded himself that the noise was the roaring of "Patience and Endurance." Immediately, he related in a letter to *The New York Times,* "the sound stopped distracting me. I have to thank the lions for my patience and endurance." And after her first visit to the Library, an eleven-year-old girl proved herself a true New Yorker, enthusing about "Patience and Attitude."

Although the Lions are New York's mascots, they stand first of all for the Library itself. By the mid-1920s, cartoonists were using them as symbols of the landmark building. Reporting on the Library's expansion plans on September 16, 1928, *The New York Times* observed, "The lions before the Public Library, pets of New York for almost a generation, are to be outflanked. Little longer can they lounge in majestic nonchalance, looking with vision unobstructed up and down the avenue. At either side of them, to the north and to the south, the library is to put out wings." (Fortunately for all concerned, this particular scheme came to naught.) The sculptures were so thoroughly identified with the Library by 1930 that *The New Yorker* drew laughs with a cartoon of two men who confused the Library's mascots with the MGM trademark.

The Library claimed the Lions as its symbol only after the public had assigned them that role. The institution used the "Revised Statuary" cartoon as the cover for one of its publications and the cubs cartoon for its 1943 Christmas card. During the '40s, its stationery carried a profile of one of the cats and the slogan "Read Between the Lions." The Library has been more fickle than the public, however. The Lions were dropped from the letterheads in the mid-'70s and graphic designers were hired to create a trendy new logo. In 1979, a Library spokesperson admitted what the public had known for decades: "We didn't need to spend hundreds of dollars on creating a corporate image [because] we already had one."

Stamp from the United States Postal Service featuring the southerly Lion, depicted by illustrator Nancy Stahl; issued on November 9, 2000.

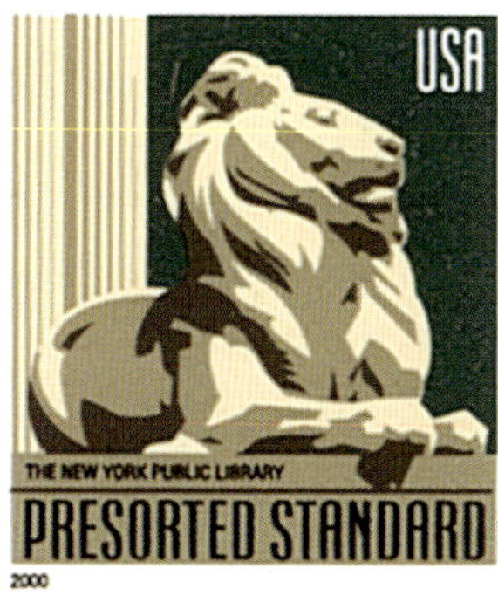

Today, the Lions are an inescapable symbol of the Library. New Yorkers see them every time they use a Library card, open a Library book, receive a letter from the institution, pick up its calendar of events, or glance at a Friends brochure. Whatever they buy in The Library Shop is placed in a bag bearing a Lion's profile. Inside the bag, a Lion may appear on a greeting card, paperweight, or T-shirt. Library patrons log into CATNYP to explore the Library's research collections, LEO to search the catalog of the circulating libraries, and PAWS for Braille or recorded books. The institution's supporters in their twenties and thirties join Young Lions; distinguished writers are honored annually as Literary Lions; and donors interested in supporting the Library's services for children enlist in the Young Cubs Program.

The early media attacks did not permanently taint the public's response to the sculptures, nor did any public relations campaign inspire their appreciation. People simply like the Lions. This affection was firmly established long before the Library began embellishing them with wreaths or reproducing them as bookends and stuffed toys. Indeed, New Yorkers' spontaneous, natural response to the big cats may make them the most genuinely popular public art in America.

Ensuring a Second Century

Tennessee pink marble, the type used for the Library Lions, is better suited to outdoor sculpture than any other, but nine decades of relentless exposure to heat and cold, moisture and drought, freezing and thawing have inevitably taken a toll. In addition, air pollution from automobile exhaust and the burning of coal and oil—all prevalent at the busy intersection of Fifth Avenue and 42nd Street—has further corroded the statues. Acid rain attacks the alkaline stone, causing decay. More troubling, it could be said that the public loves the Lions to death. Worn and polished areas betray the inadvertent abuse by the thousands of people who have ignored the prohibition against climbing on the statues.

The southerly Lion being misted with a handheld steamer, November 2004.

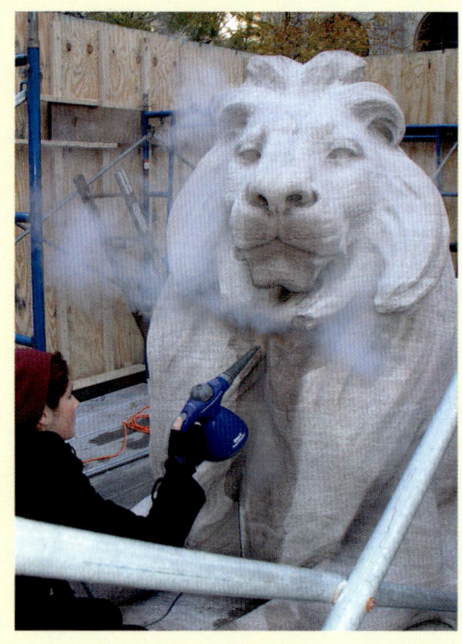

Sadly, the popular practice of decorating the big cats with wreaths and headgear also endangers them. The sculptures were first festooned with Christmas wreaths in December 1950. Ten years later, the practice was suspended because a vandal set fire to the northerly Lion's wreath, cracking his mane, chest, and a paw. The tradition was revived a few years later, using fire-resistant materials, only to be halted in 2002 because water, snow, and ice accumulated around the wreaths.

In the autumn of 1975, the Lions were cleaned with a poultice of talcum powder and cleansers, then coated with a barium hydroxide solution that created an invisible film resistant to deterioration from acid rain. They had a little work done again in 2004. For most of that November, the sculptures were hidden within blue-painted plywood enclosures while a team of conservators, led by John Griswold, restored them. Worried

New Yorkers knocked on the doors to the blue cages, demanding, "What are you doing to our lions?" Inside, the sculptures received gentle treatment. Conservators whisked them gently with nylon brushes to remove grit, grime, and pigeon droppings, then misted them with handheld steam cleaners. They rinsed away dirt, moss, and mold with a detergent that leaves no chemically active residue. To keep ice from enlarging hairline cracks, the experts injected them with grout. They removed gypsum deposits from the ears and nostrils, secured two large cracks in the northerly Lion's mane with stainless steel pins, patched them, and repointed the patch on his haunch. Completing the treatment, they cleaned and repointed the Milford Pink granite pedestals on which the Lions repose.

"Like many New Yorkers who take a respite from the city, Patience and Fortitude will return from a brief time of seclusion looking wonderfully refreshed, not noticeably altered," Library president Dr. Paul LeClerc reassured the public. Summarizing the goal of the conservation measures, he explained that the Lions "are such powerful and beloved symbols of this city, the Library wishes to preserve, improve and stabilize their integrity before any significant deterioration occurs, so they may start their second century of sitting guard in top form."

The beautifully restored southerly Lion, November 2004.

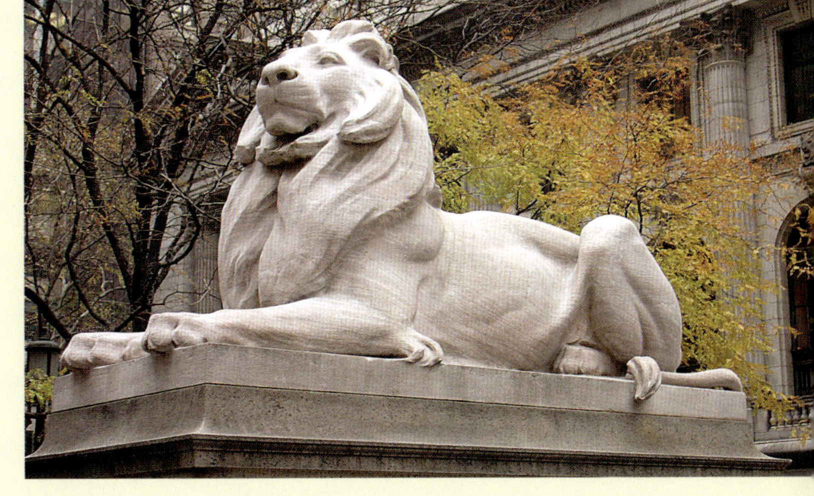

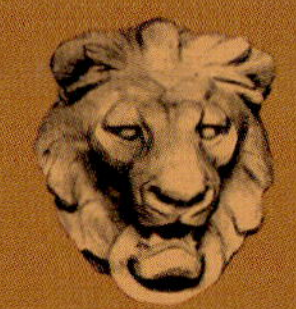

2. The Lions on Parade

THE GALLERIES THAT FOLLOW TESTIFY TO THE LIONS' enduring visual appeal. Called "New York's most lovable public sculpture" by architecture critic Paul Goldberger, they have inspired painters, printmakers, illustrators, cartoonists, and photographers. Adorned with baseball caps during the Subway Series, floral garlands in the spring, and evergreen wreaths at Christmas, they have marked the seasons in the city. Regal guardians of the passing parade, they are beginning their second century as witnesses to history.

The Lions as Fashionable Backdrops

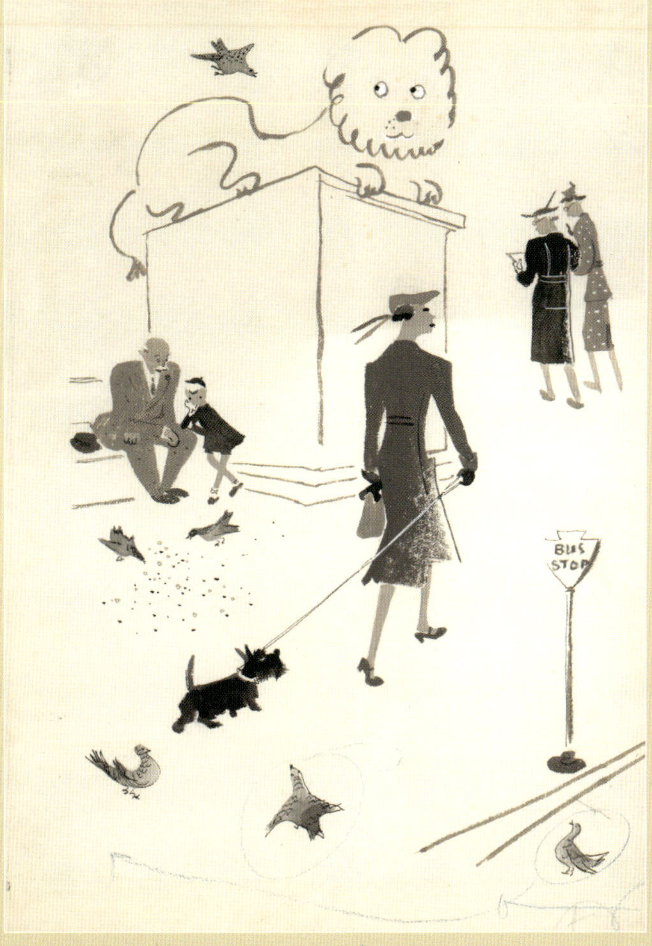

Over the years, fashion photographers and illustrators have used the Lions to convey Manhattan sophistication and style.

The original pen and ink drawing for a May 1938 print ad for B. Altman & Co., the legendary New York department store, which closed its doors in 1989.

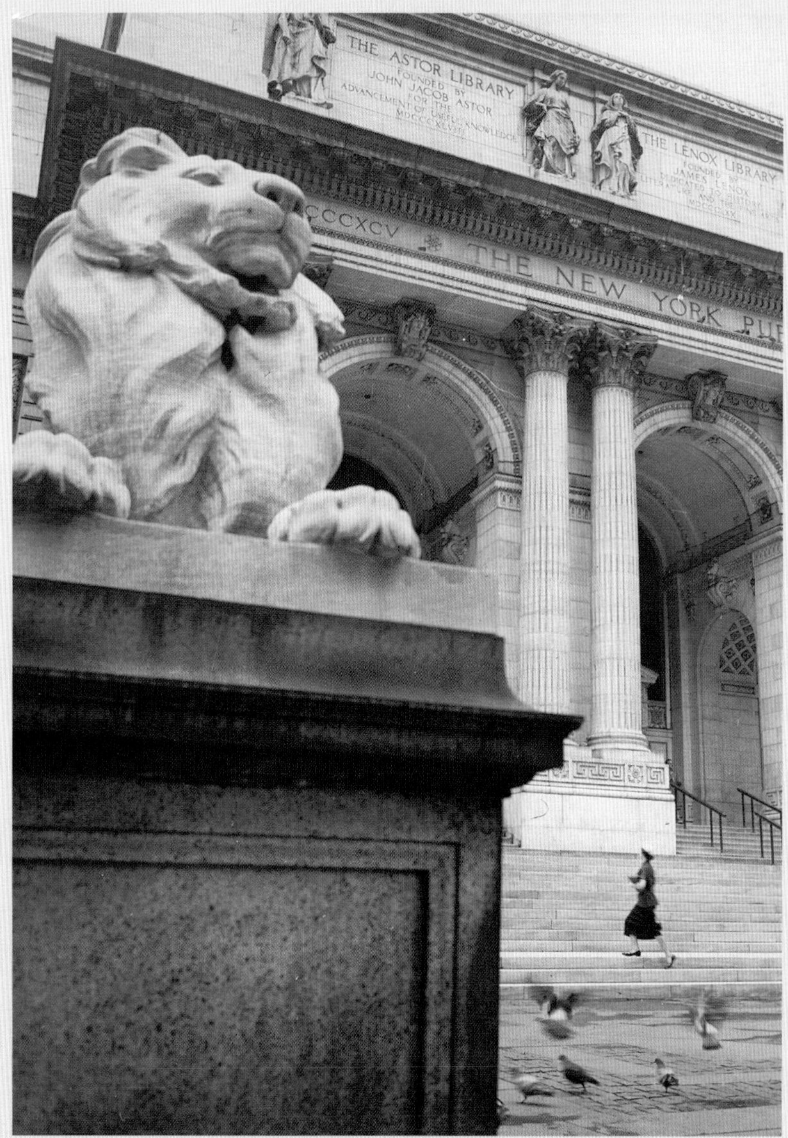

A fashion photograph by Ben Rose published in the August 1952 issue of *Seventeen* magazine.

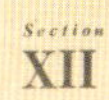

Section XII

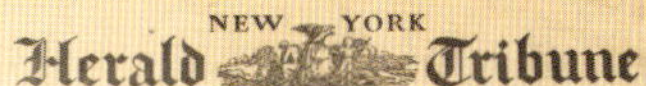

NEW YORK Herald Tribune

Section XII

EIGHT PAGES SUNDAY, MARCH 22, 1936 EIGHT PAGES

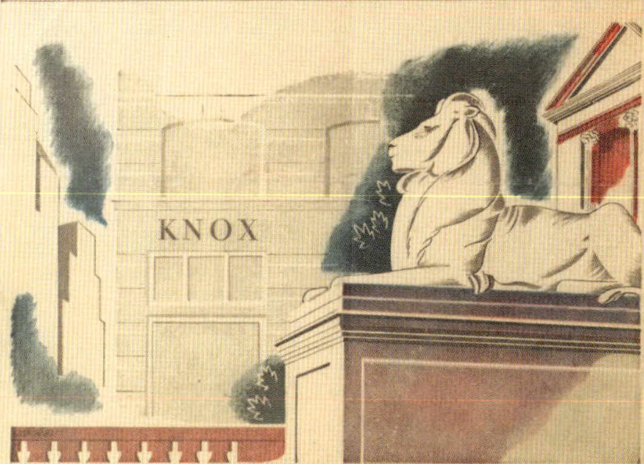

KNOX

EXPANDS...ENLARGES...REDECORATES...TO PRESENT

The Hat Corner of the World

Just Opened! The newly redecorated, enlarged Knox shop on the Avenue at Fortieth Street, south of the Public Library. Here New Yorkers will have a new introduction to The Hat Corner of the World—a collection of more fine hats than can be found in any other one place, the world over. An entire new floor provides space for larger hat and coat departments for women . . . and makes for easier shopping . . . special service.

A full-page ad for the new Knox Hat Shop at 40th Street and Fifth Avenue, just south of The New York Public Library, from the *New York Herald Tribune,* March 22, 1936.

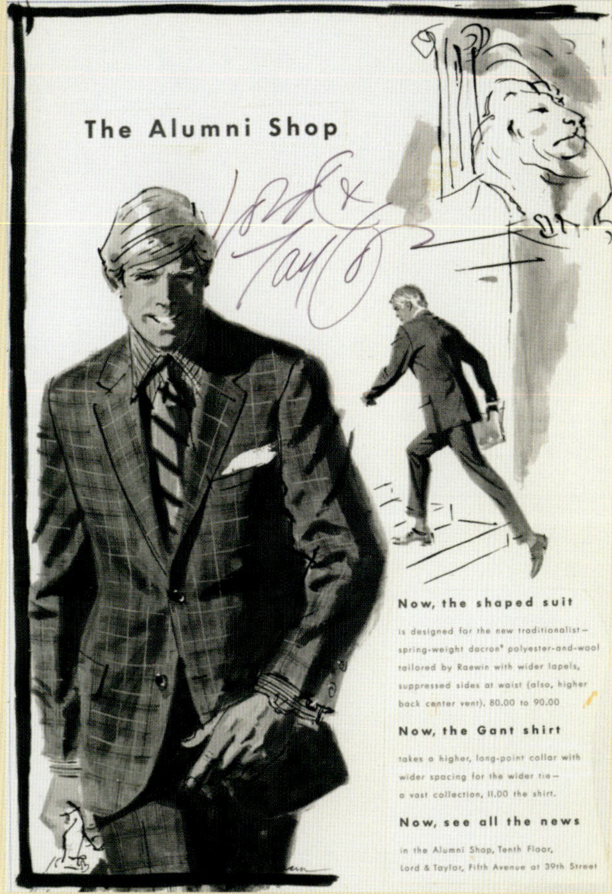

The mechanical of an advertisement for Lord & Taylor's Alumni Shop, "Drawn by L&T Artist Bob Hermann," ca. 1968.

Andy and the Lion

The New York Public Library's Spencer Collection is home to James Daugherty's original drawings for his now-classic children's tale *Andy and the Lion,* first published by The Viking Press in 1938 and named a Caldecott Honor Book the following year. A modern-day version of the fable Androcles and the Lion, *Andy and the Lion* follows the adventures of a young farm boy who loves to read—especially about lions.

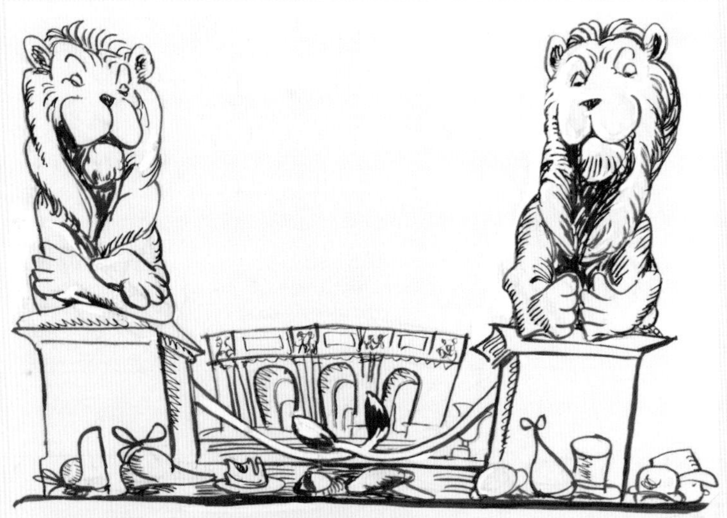

The original drawing for the dedication page of *Andy and the Lion.* Pen and ink and white gouache, ca. 1937–38. Daugherty's dedication reads: "To Lady Astor and Lord Lenox, the Library Lions who have so long sat in front of The New York Public Library and with such complacent good nature and forbearance looked down on Manhattan parade."

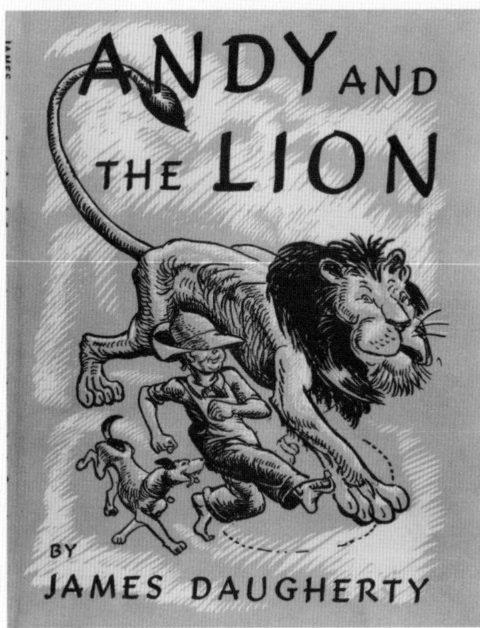

The copy of the first edition of *Andy and the Lion* that the author/artist presented to the Spencer Collection in the summer of 1938. Daugherty wrote to the chief of acquisitions at the time: "As a chronic patron of your distinguished institution over a prodigious period of time—I have always regarded those two lions which are your most outstanding and distinguishing visible feature—with great affection and esteem; to these emotions I now add that of 'pride' for they now guard in perpetuity among their sacred treasures my most distinguished work 'Andy + the Lion.' So that to me there will always be Three Library Lions."

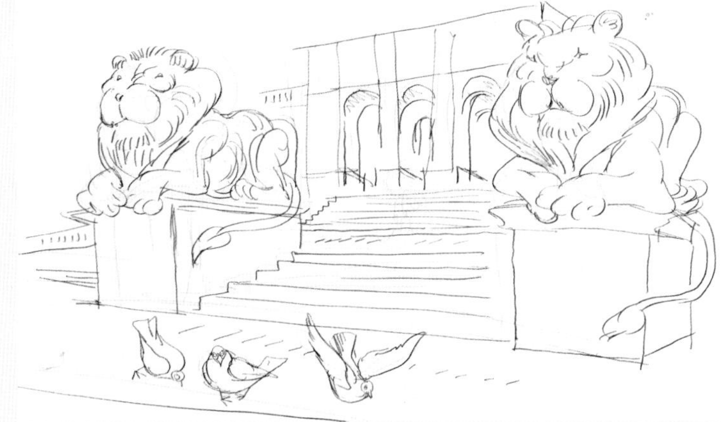

An unpublished drawing for *Andy and the Lion.* Pen and ink and graphite, ca. 1937–38.

Feeding the Lions

Cartoonists have long used the Lions to represent the Library's financial ups and downs.

A cartoon published in *Life* magazine on March 8, 1923, to mark the contribution of six million dollars to the Library's reference department by New York philanthropists Payne Whitney, Edward S. Harkness, and John D. Rockefeller, Jr.

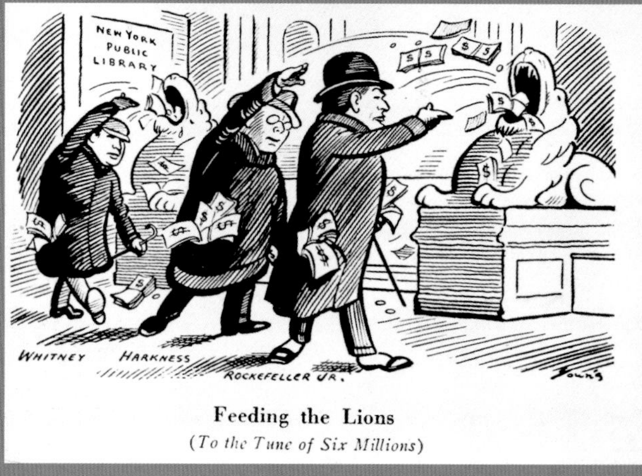

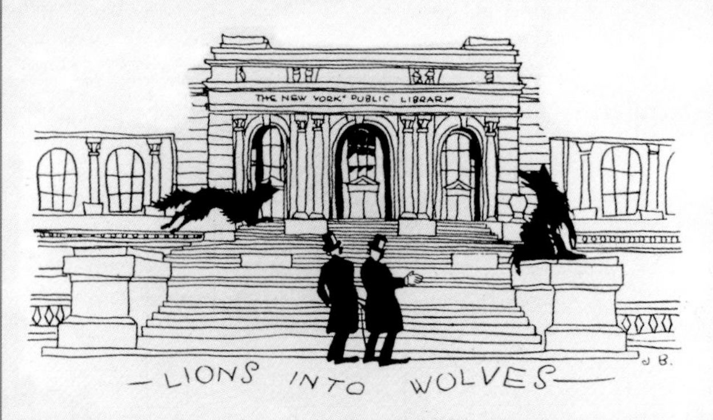

Johan Bull represented the Lions as wolves at the door of the beleaguered institution in *The New Yorker* of August 29, 1925.

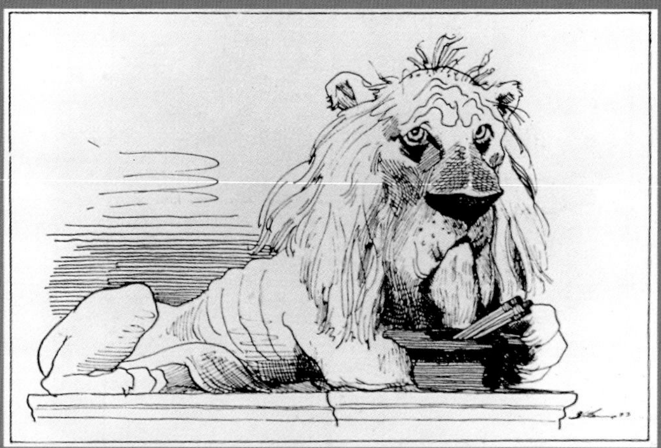

In a nod perhaps to the Great Depression, David Levine depicted an emaciated Lion reduced to selling pencils in a cartoon published in *The New York Review of Books,* May 3, 1973.

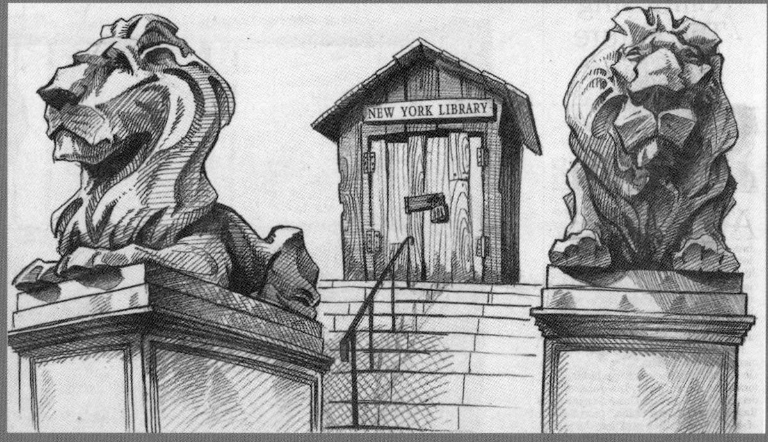

The Lions guard a padlocked, greatly diminished Library in Dav Bordeleau's drawing, which illustrated an article on proposed budget cuts to the city's library system in *The New York Sun,* May 13, 2004.

The Lions as Symbols of

The Lions have come to symbolize not just The New York Public Library but libraries and reading in general.

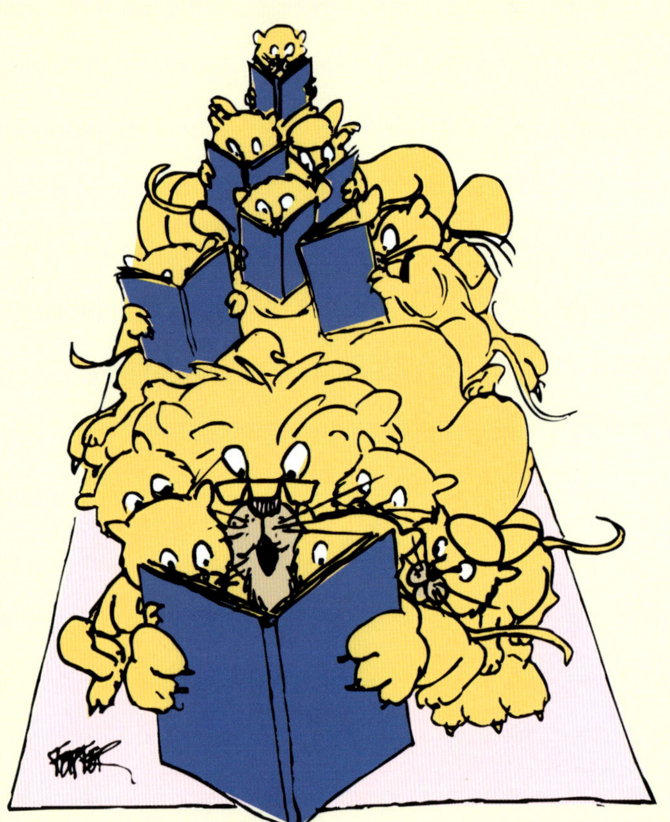

Jules Feiffer surrounded a patriarchal lion with a litter of bookish cubs in a drawing used to publicize the Library's Family Party, held on Sunday, February 24, 2002.

Libraries and Reading

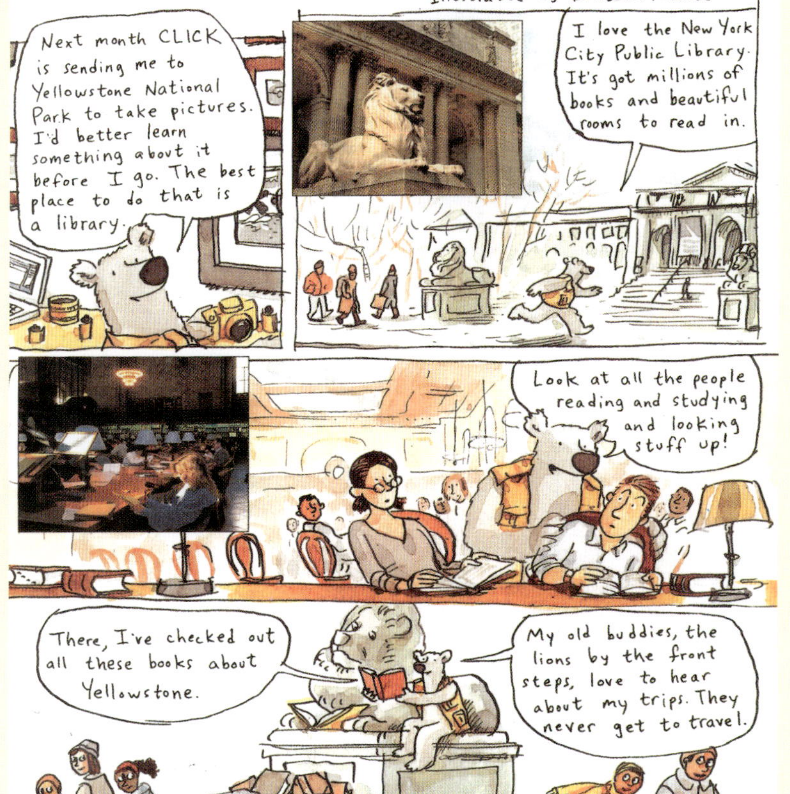

According to illustrator Brian Floca, Beatrice Black Bear is the "intrepid and charming bear photographer who appears on the back of each issue of *Click* magazine in a feature written by John Grandits and illustrated by yours truly." *Click*® is a magazine for children ages three to seven; this panel enlivened the back of the February 2005 issue.

Richard Taylor. *A Revised Statuary for the City of Tomorrow.* Original drawing in pen and ink, watercolor, and gouache; published in *The New Yorker,* October 15, 1938.

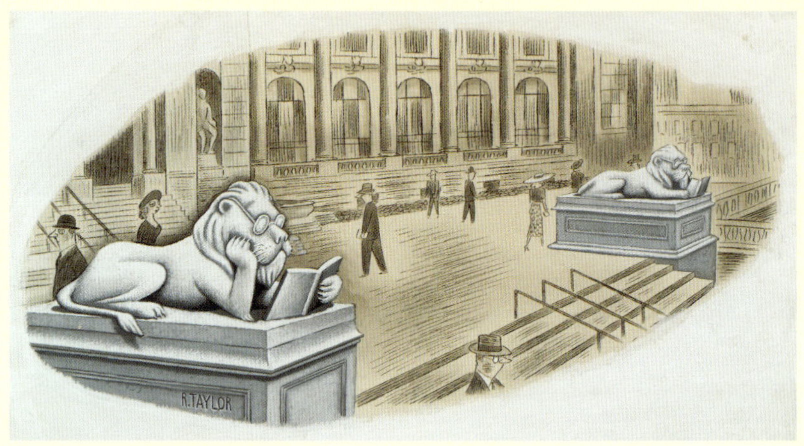

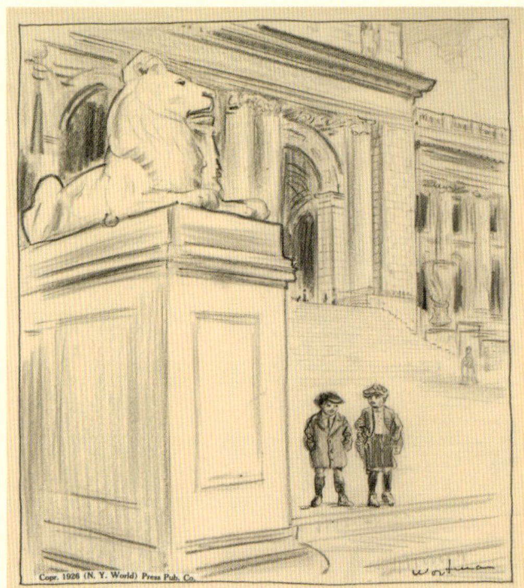

"Outside of that cowboy book I showed you, there ain't a decent book in the whole library."

Denys Wortman. Original ink and graphite drawing; published in *The New York World* in 1926.

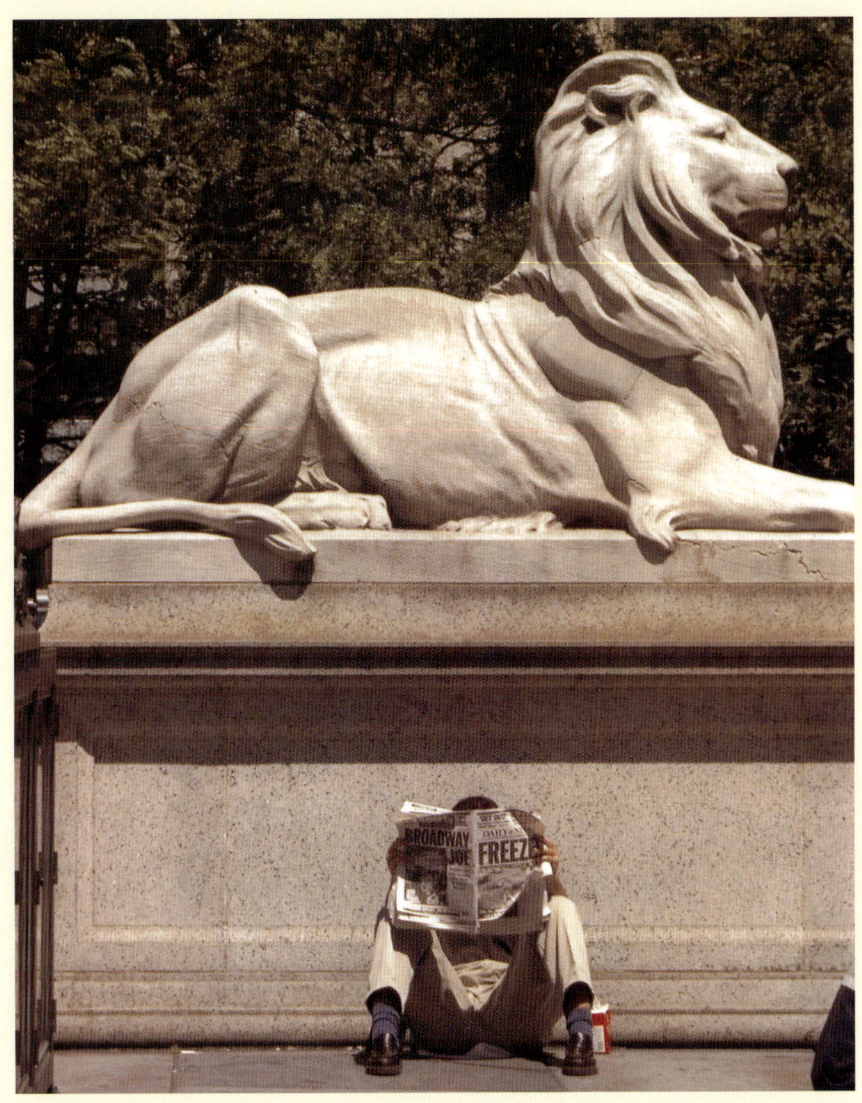

The northerly Lion's pedestal offers support to a man perusing one of New York City's tabloids.

Cartoon Celebrities: The New Yorker's Lions

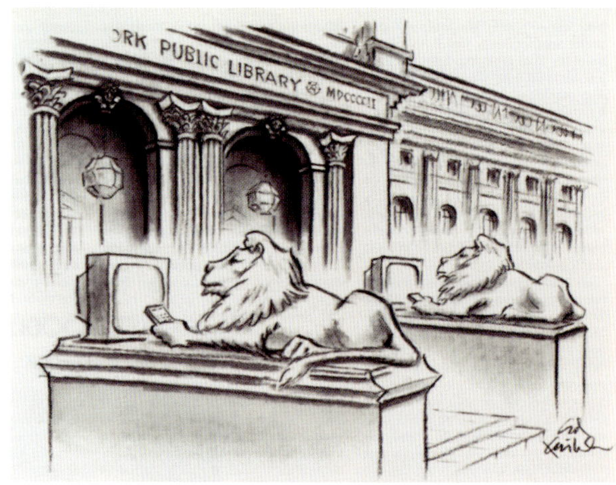

Ed Fisher. Published in *The New Yorker,* February 1, 1993.

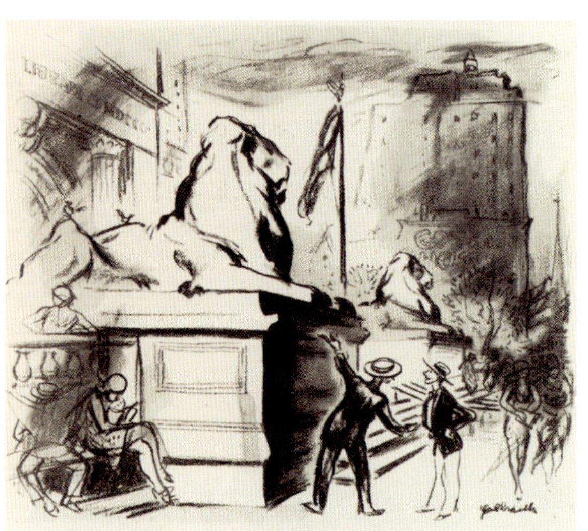

"Let's go in here. Metro-Goldwyn pictures are always good."

William Crawford Galbraith. Published in *The New Yorker,* May 24, 1930.

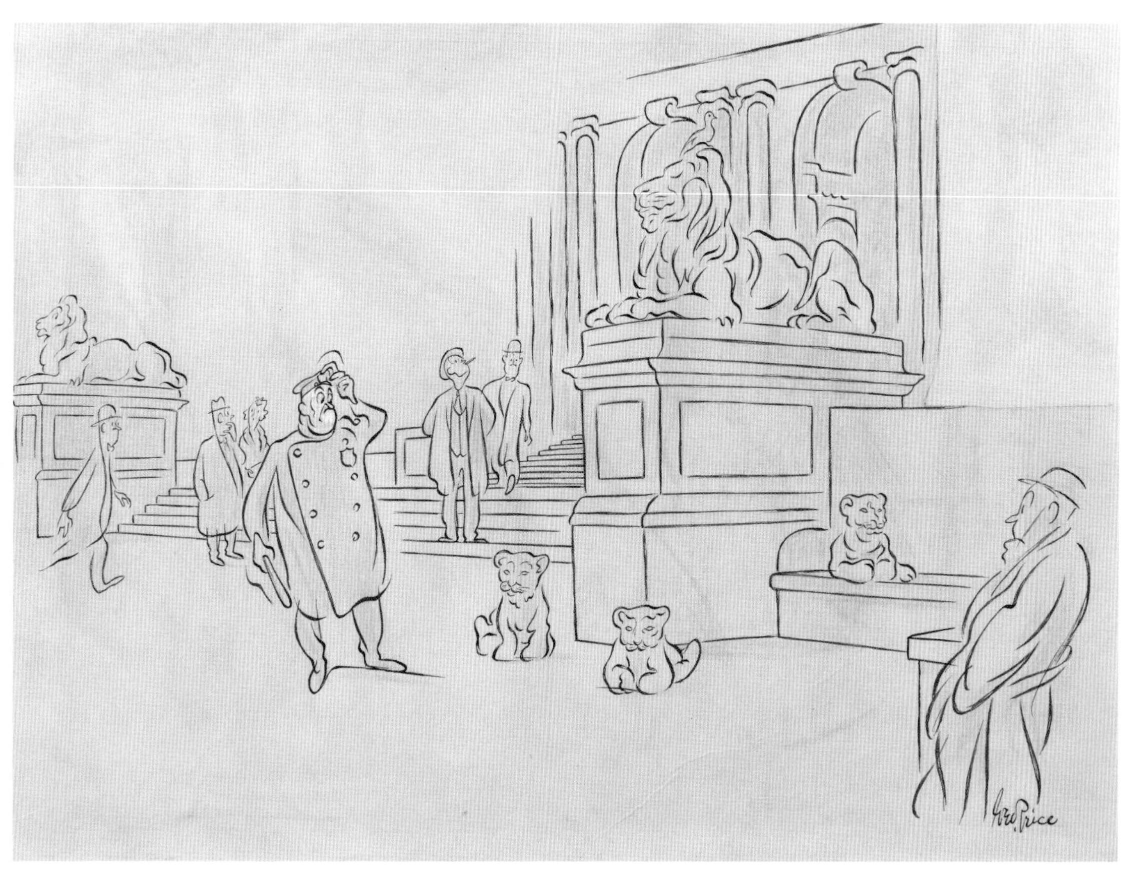

George Price. Original drawing in ink and blue pencil, 1935; published in *The New Yorker,* March 2, 1935.

The Lions Adorned

The sight of the snooty lions decked out in headgear or wreaths elicits a smile from visitors and even the most blasé New Yorkers.

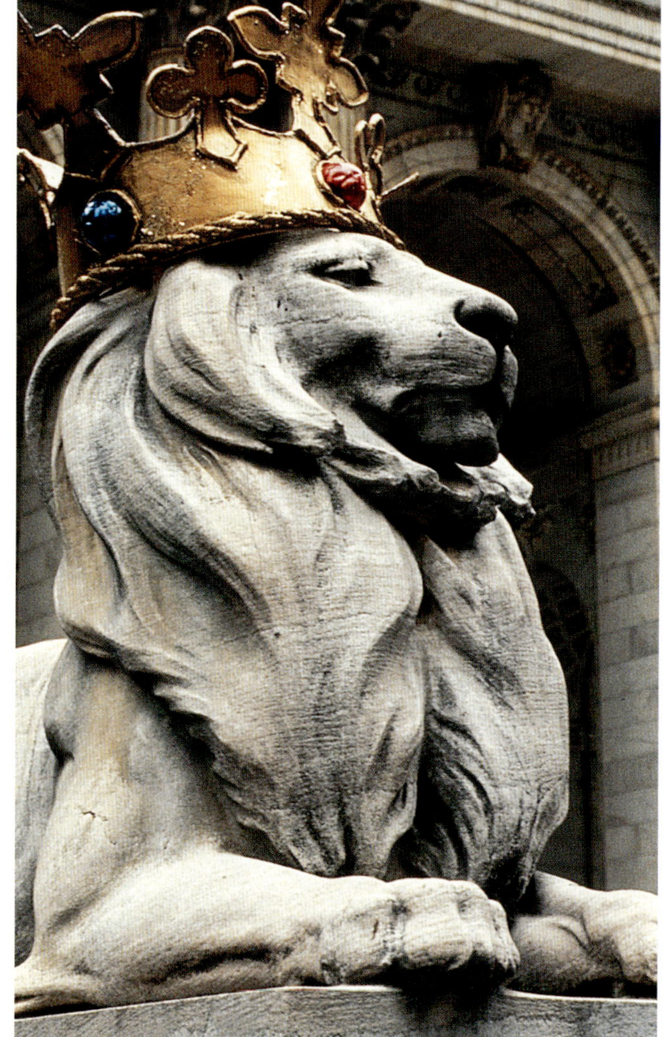

A majestically crowned Lion promotes the exhibition *King Arthur: Looking at the Legend* in 1991–92.

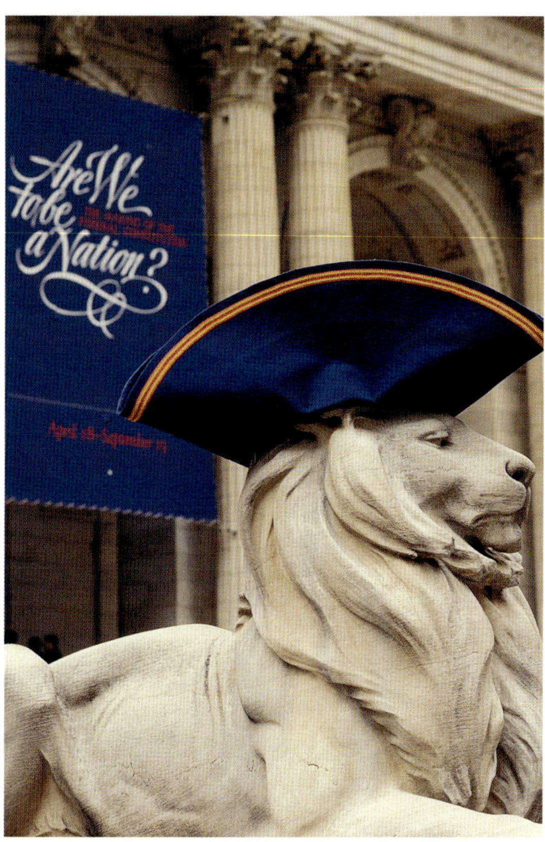

A Lion in a blue tricorn hat marks the exhibition *Are We to Be a Nation? The Making of the Federal Constitution* in 1987.

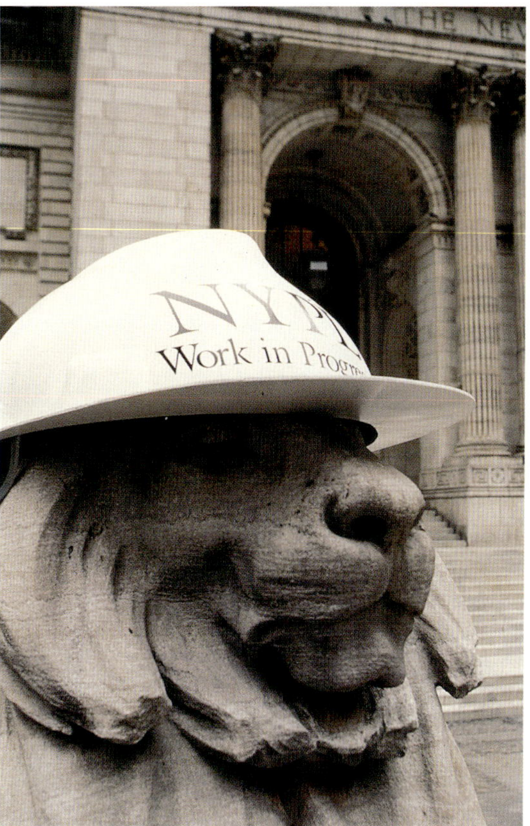

The southerly Lion topped with a fifty-pound hard hat, September 18, 1997, heralding the "Second Century Campaign" for NYPL's libraries and a major renovation of the landmark building at 42nd Street and Fifth Avenue.

The southerly Lion in top hat and black tie celebrates the 75th anniversary of The New York Public Library's Central Building at Fifth Avenue and 42nd Street (now known as the Humanities and Social Sciences Library), May 1986.

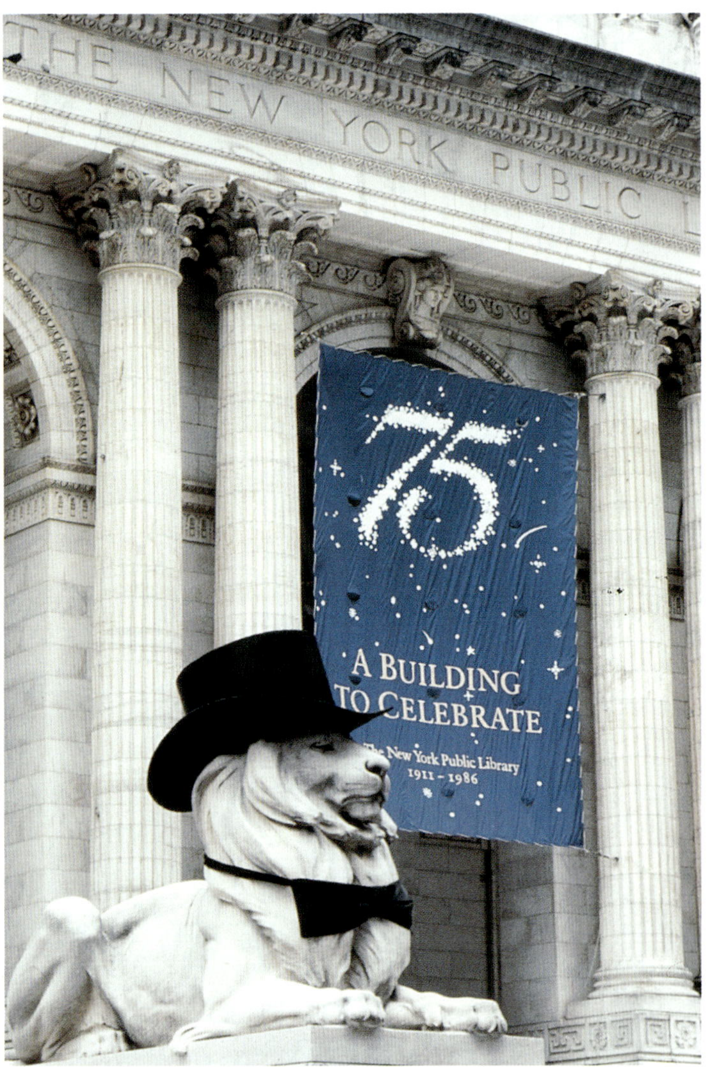

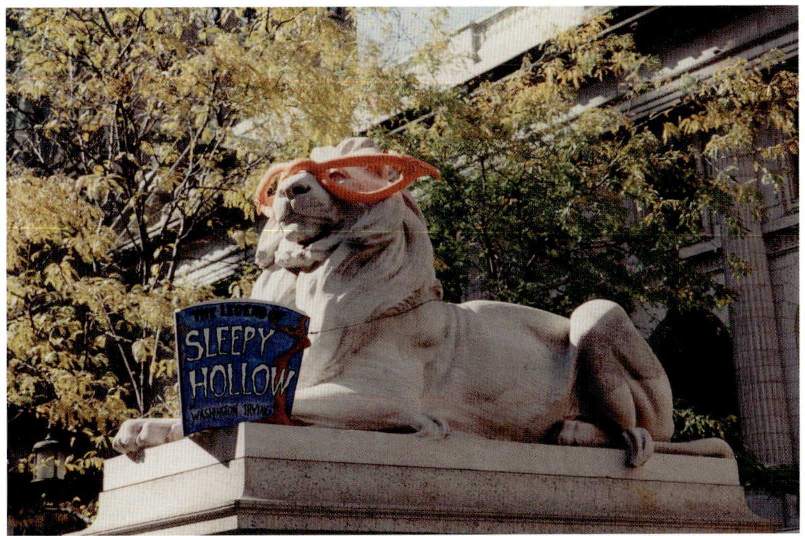

Patience gets in the mood for Halloween by reading *The Legend of Sleepy Hollow,* while Fortitude is engrossed in *The Raven,* October 1993. Designed by Debby Lee Cohen.

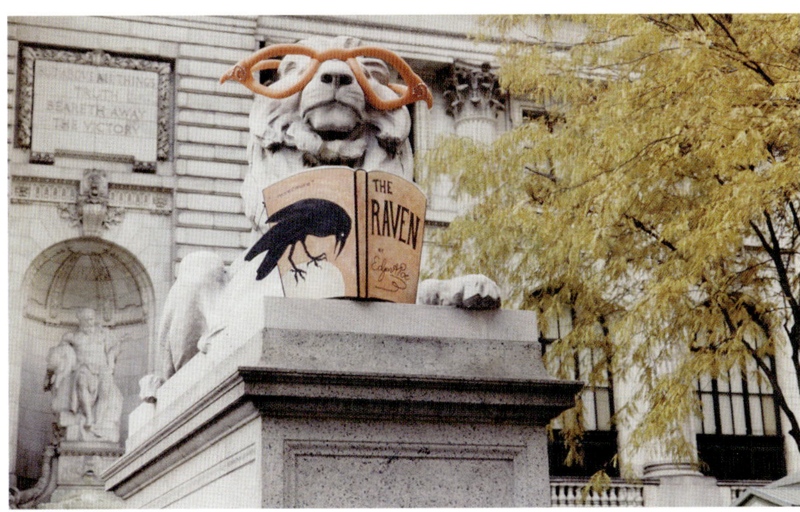

On the Cover:

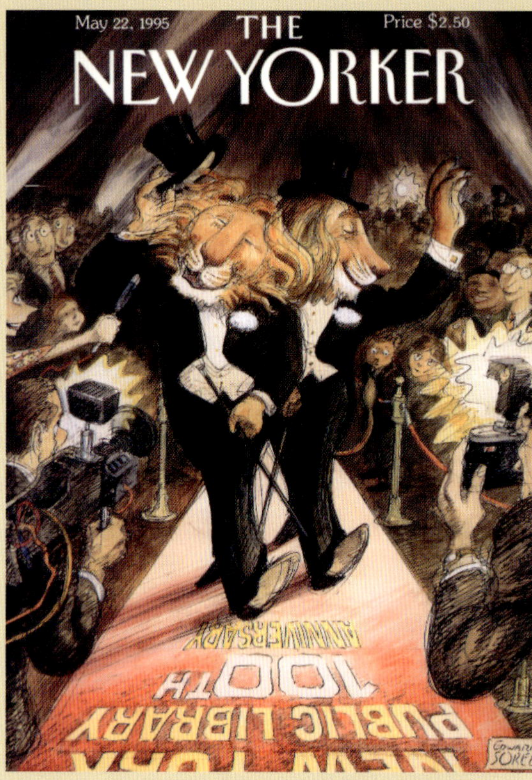

Edward Sorel, *The Roar of the Crowd,* celebrating the Library's Centennial, May 22, 1995.

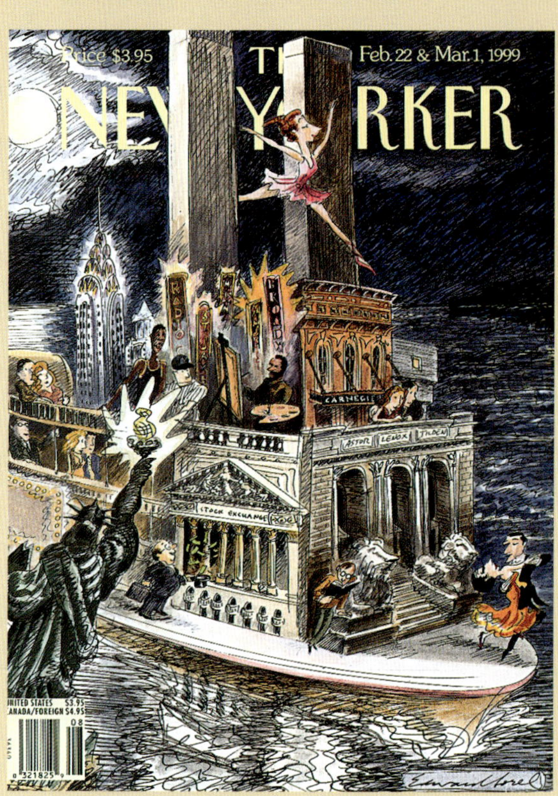

Edward Sorel, *City of Dreams,* February 22 and March 1, 1999.

The New Yorker's Lions

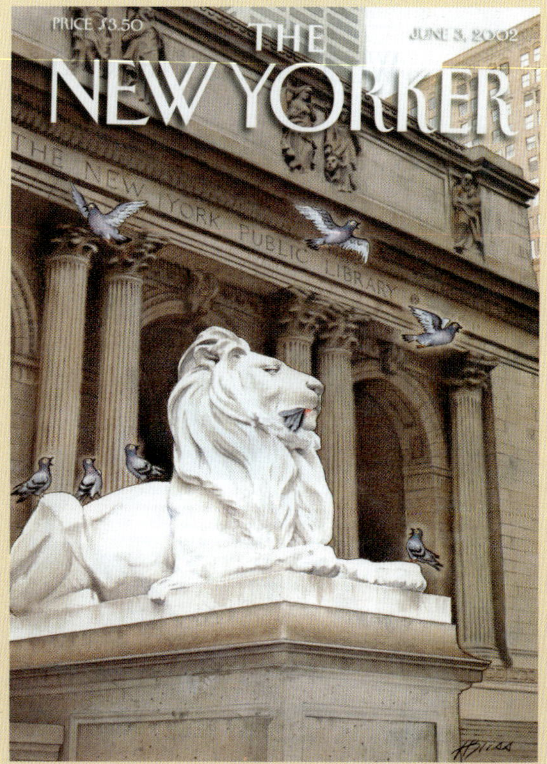

Harry Bliss, *It's a Jungle Out There,* June 3, 2002.

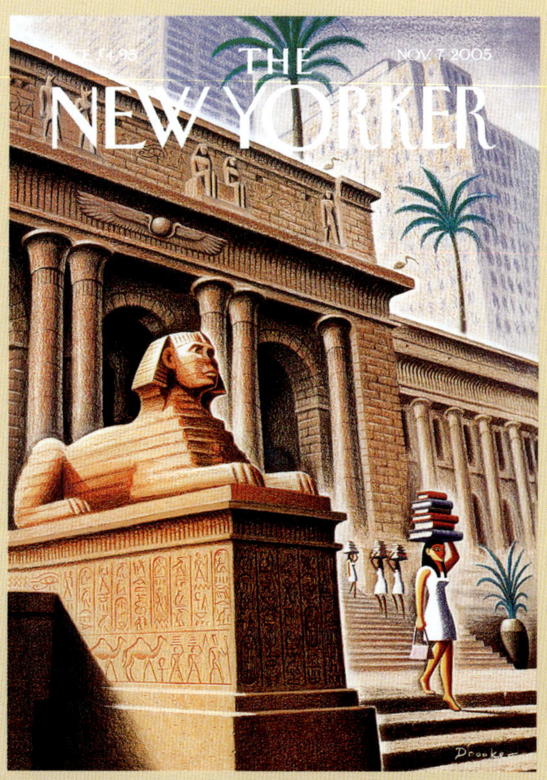

Eric Drooker, *Arcane Pleasures,* November 7, 2005.

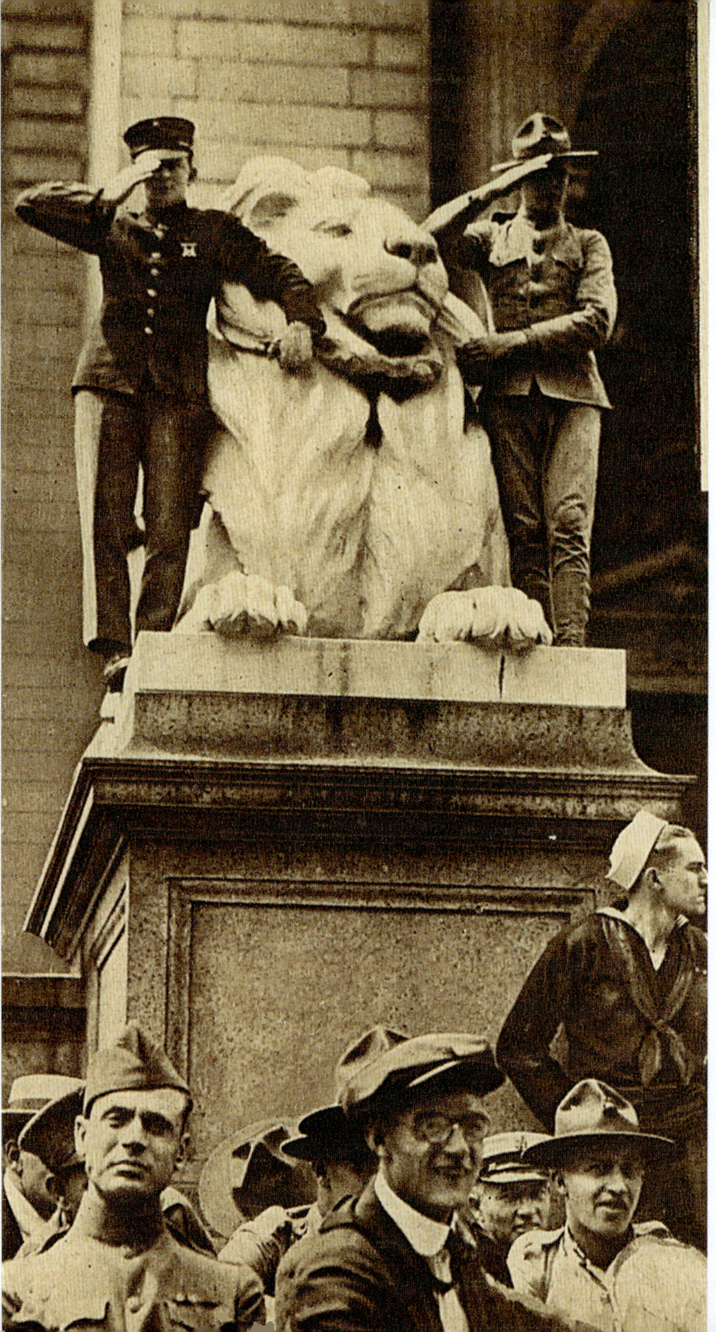

The Lions

Two Marines climbed onto the southerly Lion's plinth to salute their returning comrades in the Second Division as a welcome parade for the legendary World War I combat unit passed the reviewing stand in front of the Library, August 8, 1919. Marchers and civilians cheered the more than five hundred wounded veterans who were seated near the reviewing stand.

as Witnesses to History

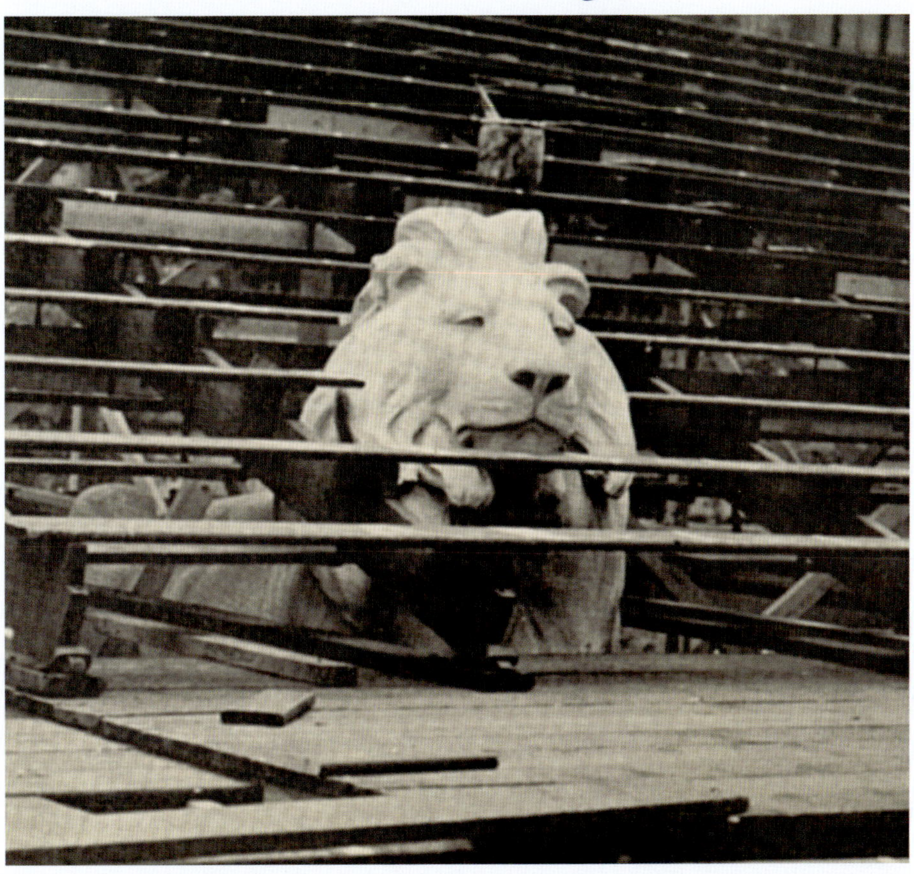

In for the Duration, or, the Library in Wartime. **A Library Lion looks out through the reviewing stand for the New York in the War Parade, June 13, 1942.**

On June 19, 1945, more than four million New Yorkers turned out to cheer General Dwight D. Eisenhower, the supreme commander of the Allied Expeditionary Force in World War II, as he made a victory procession through the jammed streets of the city. As the *Times* reported the next day, "A homespun American from the plains of Kansas came back from the wars yesterday to a triumph such as Rome never gave a conquering Caesar."

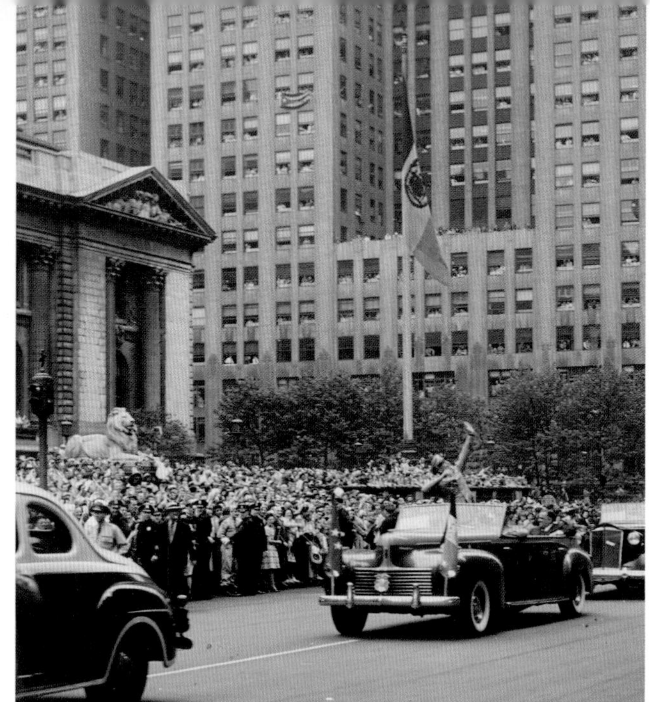

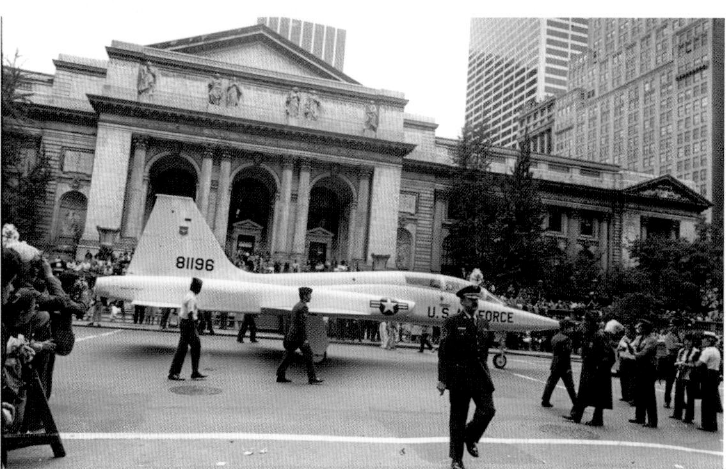

Photograph by Robert Sefcik, 1981.

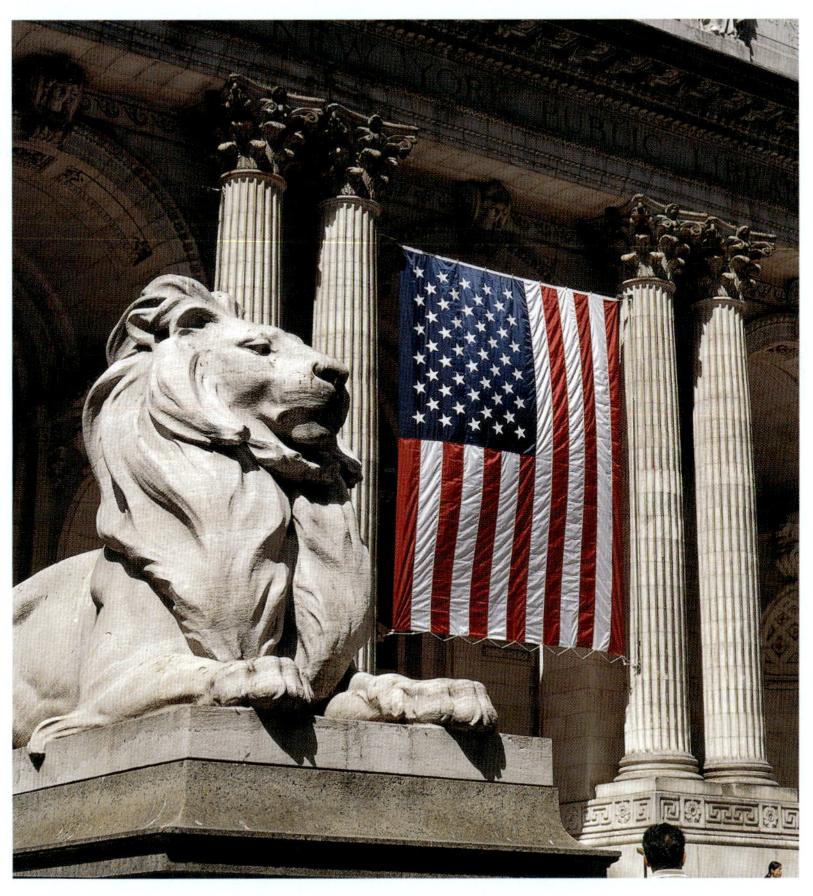

September 11, 2002, marking the first anniversary of 9/11.

The Lions in Winter

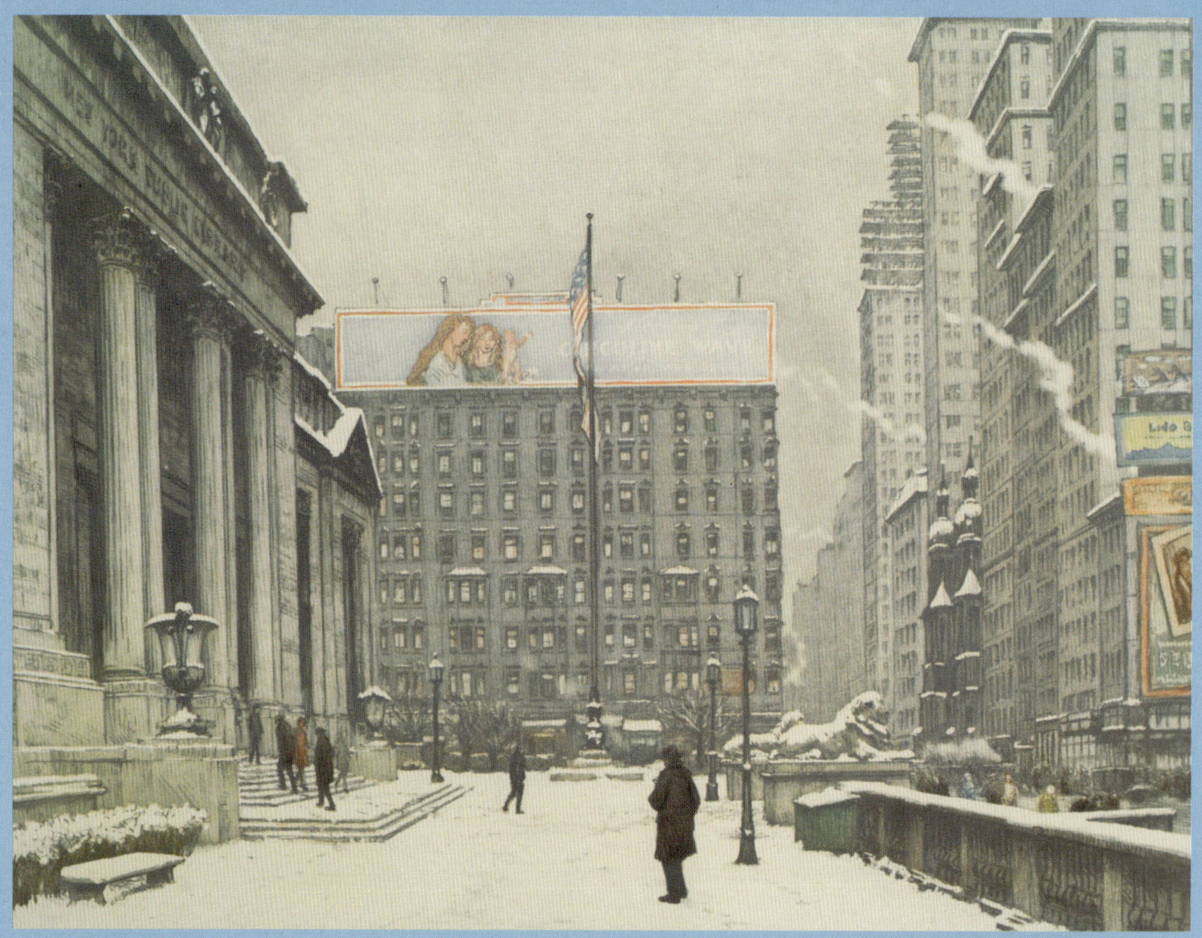

Tavik Frantisek Šimon. *New York Public Library.* Color soft-ground and aquatint, 1927.

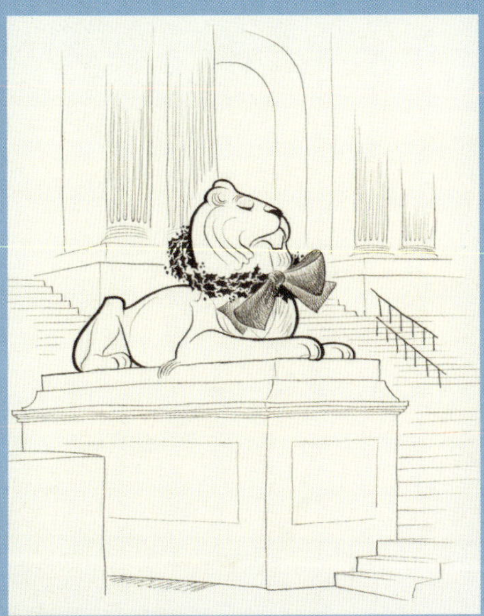

Al Hirschfeld, *House of the Lions.* Original india ink drawing, 1954; published in Oriana Atkinson's *Manhattan and Me* (1954), with "Drawings by Hirschfeld." This illustration appeared at the head of the "House of the Lions" chapter, Atkinson's affectionate (and droll) tribute to The New York Public Library. Of the Lions, she writes: "Nowadays they are the darlings of New York. . . . As the years have passed the dreamy beasts have become not only famous but beloved. They have somehow come to represent the spirit of the city. They are tolerant, if terrible; they are powerful, but benign and a little mocking."

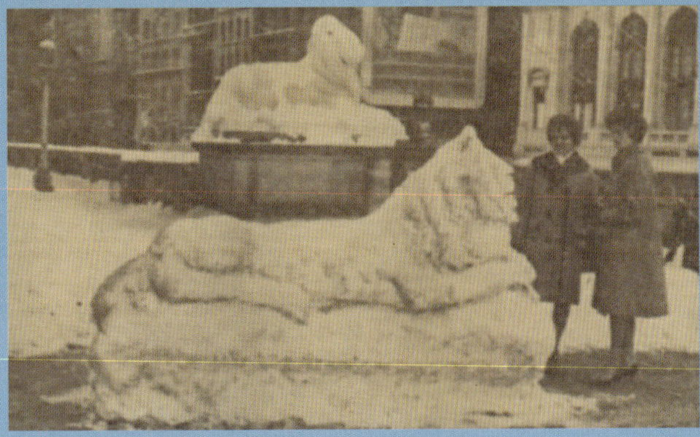

From *The New York Standard,* January 27, 1963. The original caption read: "And Then There Were Three: This is a chilly tale of trolls in the night. As the temperature dipped to the teens, persons unknown, and presumably unseen, stole onto the promenade of the New York Public Library at 42nd St. and Fifth Ave. Braving frigid winds, they added a third lion to the famous two library guardians. True, the new addition is only of snow, but the pleasure is all Manhattan's. Alas, comes the thaw, three lions will again be two."

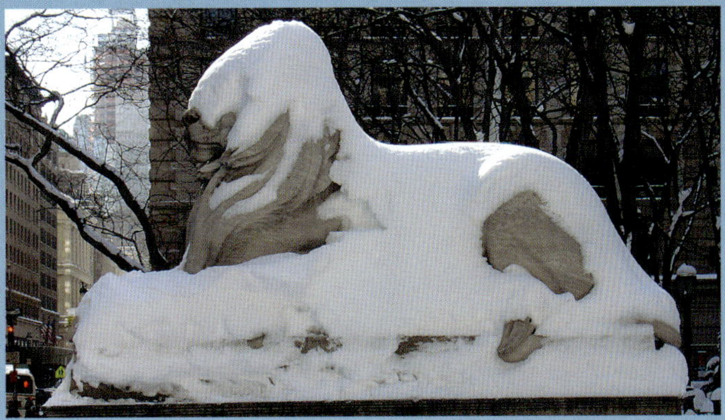

A Library Lion blanketed in snow, on February 14, 2006, the morning after what the *New York Post* dubbed "The Great Whiteout of '06" dumped 26.9 inches of snow on New York City. It was, said the *Post,* "the biggest, boldest, baddest snowstorm ever to bombard the city."

The Lions Come to Life

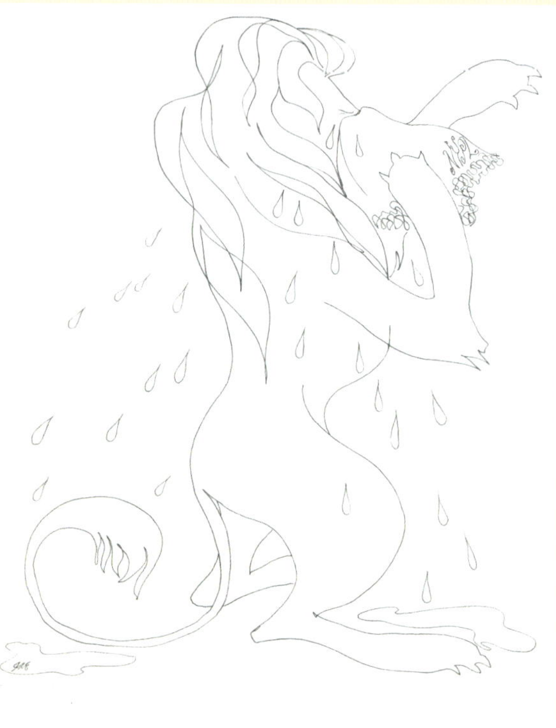

This drawing by the abstract painter Jimmy Ernst, son of Dadaist Max Ernst and, with his wife, Edith, a longtime benefactor of the Library, was featured on the cover of the menu for the farewell dinner held in January 1971 for Edward Geier Freehafer, director of The New York Public Library, 1954–1971. Note the NYPL monogram on the weeping Lion's handkerchief.

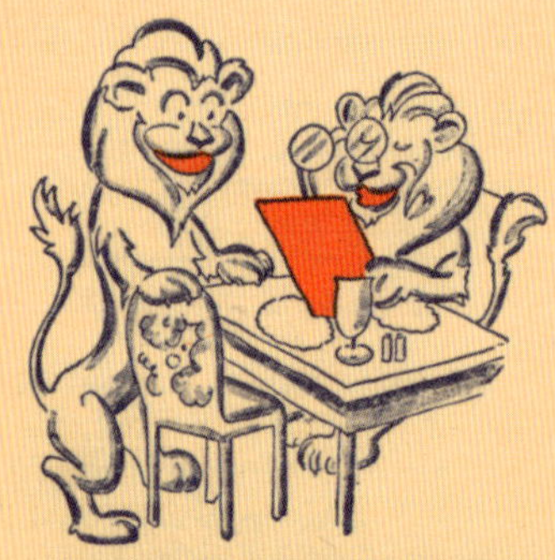

The Library Lions Lunching
at
ROSE MARIE

The Lions are ordering their noon-day SNACK of high-calory soup, platter of juicy meat and two fresh green vegetables, plump home-made hot rolls, dessert and coffee. (Tariff, 50c. to 75c., to Lions and all others.)

Note Mrs. Lion's expression. Her lorgnette has just lighted on her favorite apple pie with cheese crust, one of the daily dessert-delights at Rose Marie. She is literally roaring for it.

Both of them declare that the Lion's share of fine food is served at Rose Marie; they should know. . .they've lunched nowhere else for eleven years.

Mrs. Ames selects the food and supervises the cooking of every bite served at Rose Marie. She personally makes the pastries and hot breads. Nowhere else in the neighborhood will you find true home cooking in the real (not road-side) sense. Luncheons, 50c. to 75c. Dinners, 75c. to $1.00.

For moderate a la carte prices, peruse the attached menu.

Handbill for Rose Marie, a restaurant formerly located at 17 East 41st Street, just a few steps east of the Library, ca. 1940. On the verso, it is noted, "If you should miss the Lions from the front of the Library—they're probably at the Rose Marie."

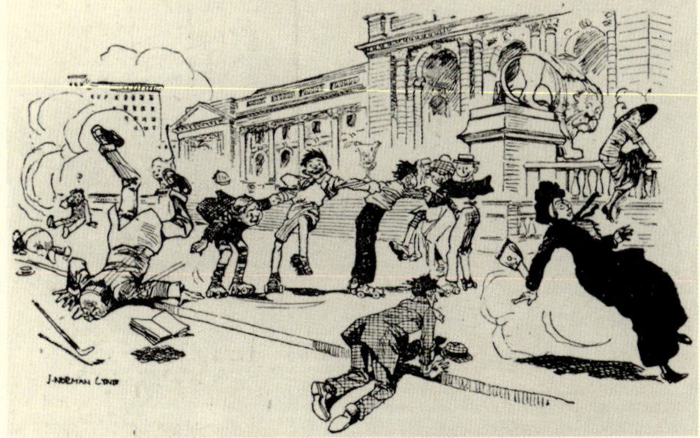

In this early cartoon featuring the Library Lions, published in the *New York Herald,* September 28, 1911, J. Norman Lynd documented the rowdy shenanigans of the "swift rolling squadrons" who cause "pedestrians to rush to cover in doorways" at their appearance, as these so-called "juvenile joy riders . . . *snap the whip* on stragglers, dragging them away in captivity, with garments in disarray."

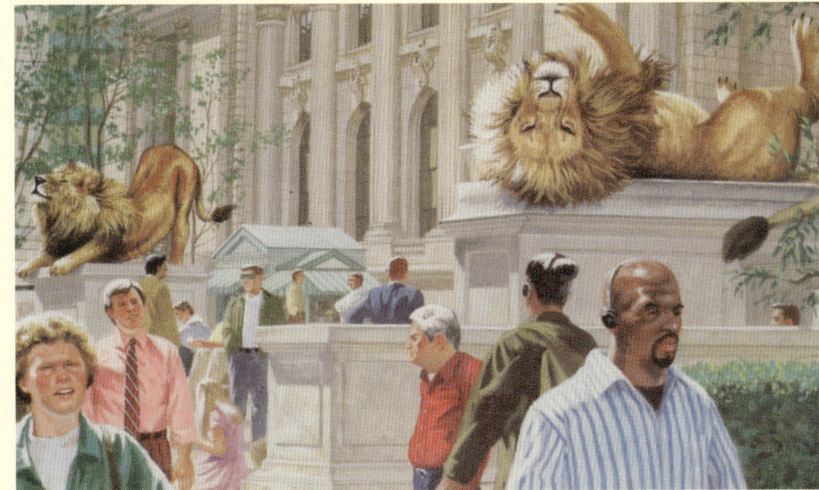

Headlined *It Takes a Hell of a Lot to Surprise New Yorkers,* this scene was featured in a 1998 print advertisement for Time Warner Cable of New York.

Urban Neighbors: The Lions

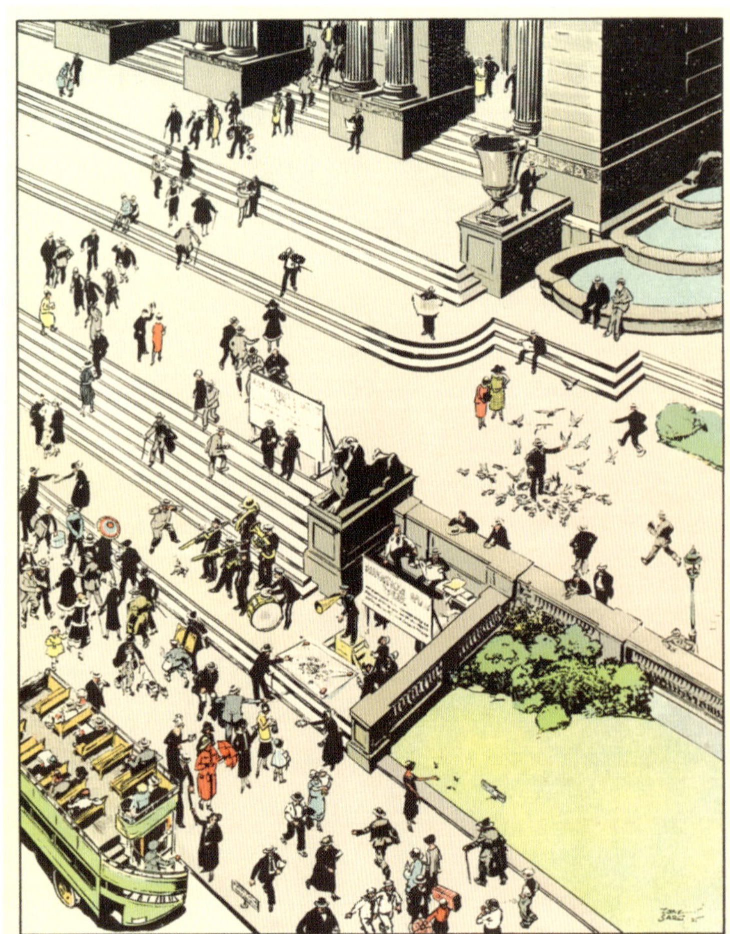

Tony Sarg. *Public Library.* Plate 2 in *Tony Sarg's New York,* a collection of the artist's bird's-eye views of the city published in 1926. Captioned "The literary center of the metropolis," this plate captures the always lively scene on the steps and terrace in front of the Library, reflecting Sarg's belief that New York should be depicted in terms of people, that "never-ending procession of . . . all kinds, from every walk of life—people who are the actors in an infinity of small comedies."

in the City

Stan Lichens.
The New York Public Library.
Photograph, 1999.

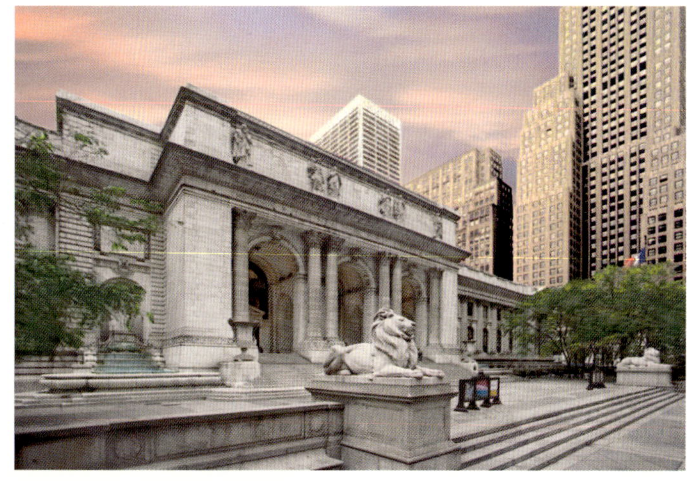

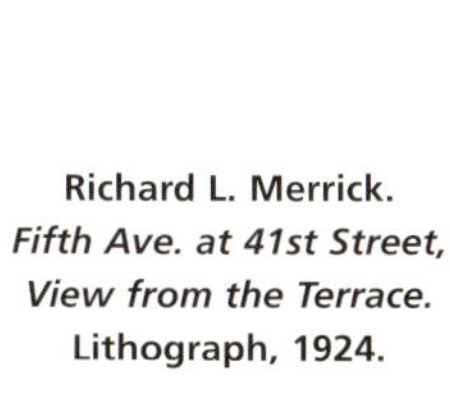

Richard L. Merrick.
Fifth Ave. at 41st Street, View from the Terrace.
Lithograph, 1924.

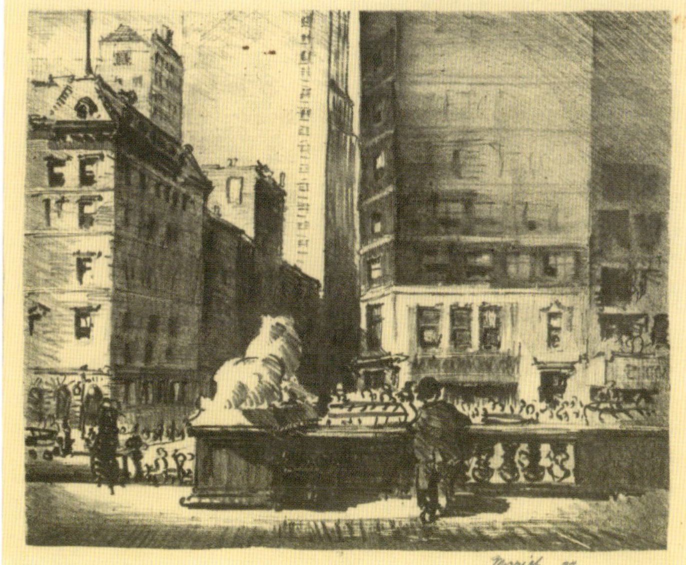

Ben Asen. *Pigeon on New York Public Library Lion.*
Photograph, December 2001.

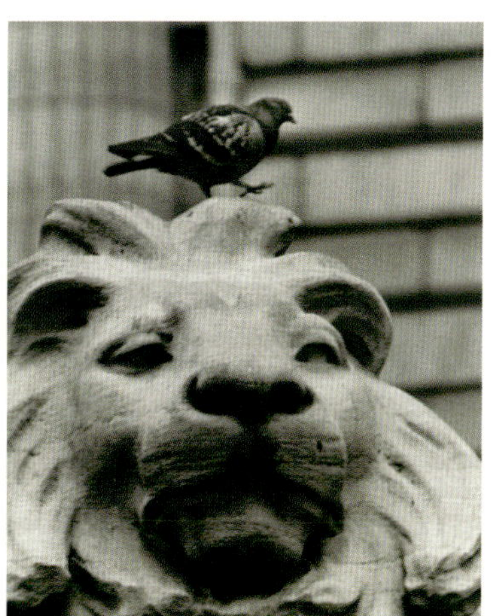

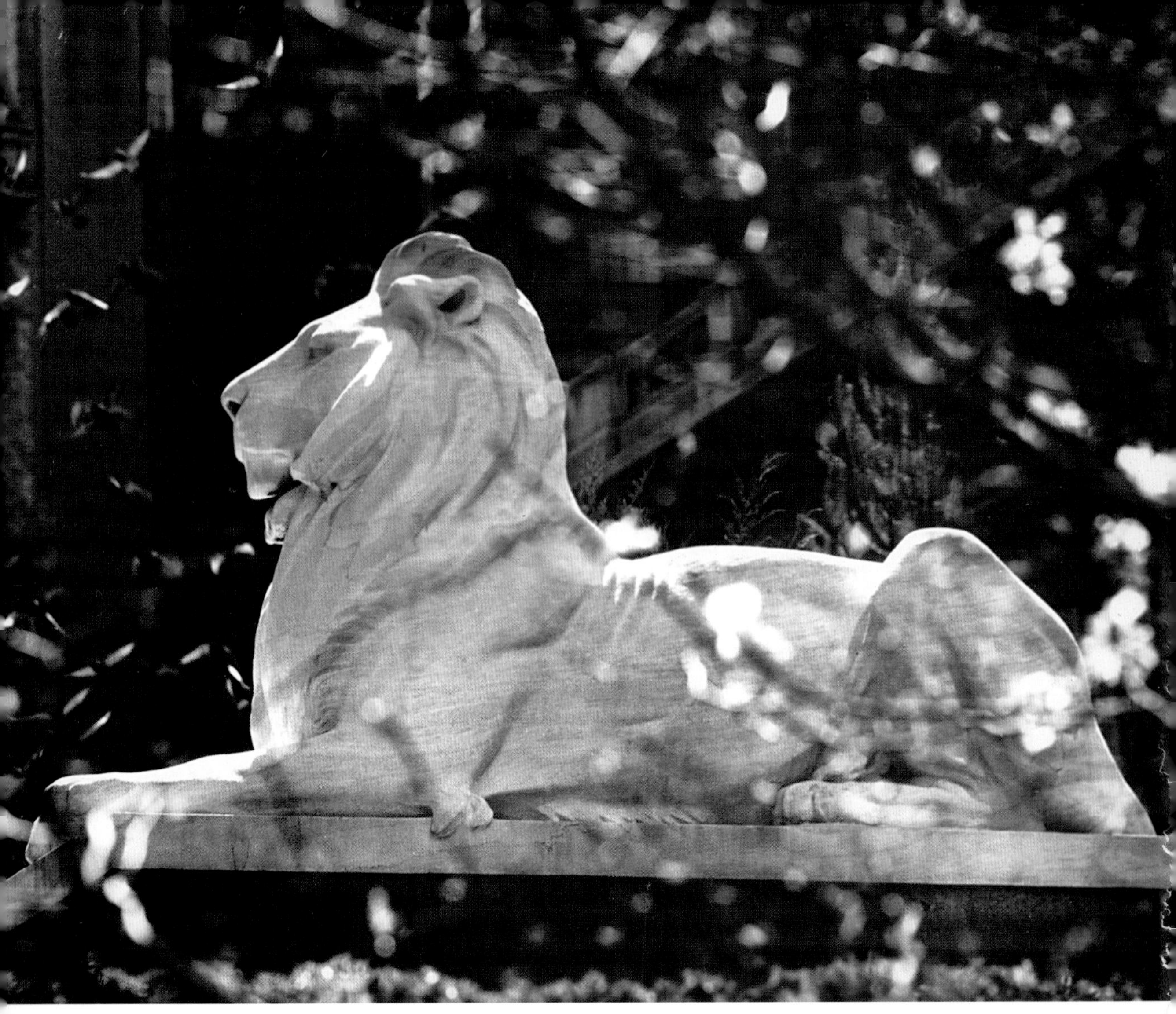

A sun-dappled Library Lion on a breezy day, ca. 1960s.

Author's Acknowledgments

Special thanks go to Mary Shelley and Bill Carroll, experts on the Piccirilli brothers; Thayer Tolles, The Metropolitan Museum of Art; Maria Cocchiarelli, Italian American Museum; Maura Eichner, SSND; Dr. Paula Henderson; Dr. Marlene Park, who stimulated my interest in public sculpture with an excellent course at the Graduate Center of the City University of New York; and Sally Webster and Harriet Senie, editors of the anthology in which my first essay on the Library Lions appeared. I am also grateful to Karen Van Westering and Anne Skillion of The New York Public Library's Publications Office and especially to editor Kenneth Benson, who sought out the best possible illustrations.

Further Reading

Adams, Adeline. "A Family of Sculptors." *The American Magazine of Art* 12 (July 1921): 223–30. A contemporary evaluation of the Piccirilli brothers, with a description of their Bronx studio.

Bertram, Brian. *Lions*. Stillwater, MN: Voyageur Press, 1998. An authoritative and well-illustrated introduction to the "King of the Beasts."

Dain, Phyllis. *The New York Public Library: A History of Its Founding and Early Years*. New York: The New York Public Library, Astor, Lenox and Tilden Foundations, 1972. A thoroughly documented history of the early Library and its predecessor institutions, described in a social and political context.

———. *The New York Public Library: A Universe of Knowledge*. New York and London: The New York Public Library/Scala Publishers, 2000. An illustrated history of the Library, from its founding in 1895 to 2000.

Denis-Huot, Christine and Michel. *The Art of Being a Lion*. New York: Friedman/Fairfax, 2002. Provides background on the lion theme in art, photographs of lions in the wild, and information about lion behavior.

Lanier, Henry Wysham. "The Sculpture of E. C. Potter." *World's Work* 12 (September 1906): 7968–81. The most important contemporary source of information on the sculptor, with illustrations of many of his early works.

Larkin, Susan G. "Edward Clark Potter and the Vagaries of Fame: A Tale of Two Sculptures." *Greenwich* 47 (March 1994): 51–54, 57–60. A comparison of the changing public response to the Library Lions and Potter's last public commission, the Bolling Memorial in Greenwich, Connecticut.

———. "From Scapegoats to Mascots: The New York Public Library Lions." In *Critical Issues in Public Art: Content, Context, and Controversy*, edited by Harriet F. Senie and Sally Webster. New York: IconEditions, 1992. The author's first essay (footnoted) on the Library Lions.

Olds, N. S. "The Stroller." *The Villager*, December 9, 1948, p. 20, and January 6, 1949, p. 16. After Olds wrote an appreciative column about the Lions in 1948, he received a letter from the sculptor's friend Henry Wysham Lanier providing insights into the creation and initial criticism of the Lions.

Potter, Edward Clark. Papers, 1866, 1890–1923. The New York Public Library, Manuscripts and Archives Division, New York. An essential resource for researchers, this includes letters, some photographs, lists of sculptures, and other materials.

———. Papers, 1903–1933. Archives of American Art, Smithsonian Institution, Washington, DC. Valuable resource for further research on the sculptor.

Shelley, Mary, and Bill Carroll. "The Piccirilli Studio." *The Bronx County Historical Society Journal* 36 (Spring 1999): 1–12. An expanded version of this essay is included, along with much else, on a Web site (built by Shelley and Carroll) devoted to the Piccirillis: http://www2.riverdale.edu/~bcarroll

Steffensen, Ingrid. *The New York Public Library: A Beaux-Arts Landmark*. London: Scala, 2003. A heavily illustrated pocket-sized guide to the architecture and ornamentation of the Humanities and Social Sciences Library, home of the Lions.

Taft, Lorado. *The History of American Sculpture*. New York: Macmillan, 1930. The first survey of its field, originally published in 1903. The 1930 edition includes an evaluation of Potter's work (pp. 474–75) and an appreciation added after his death.

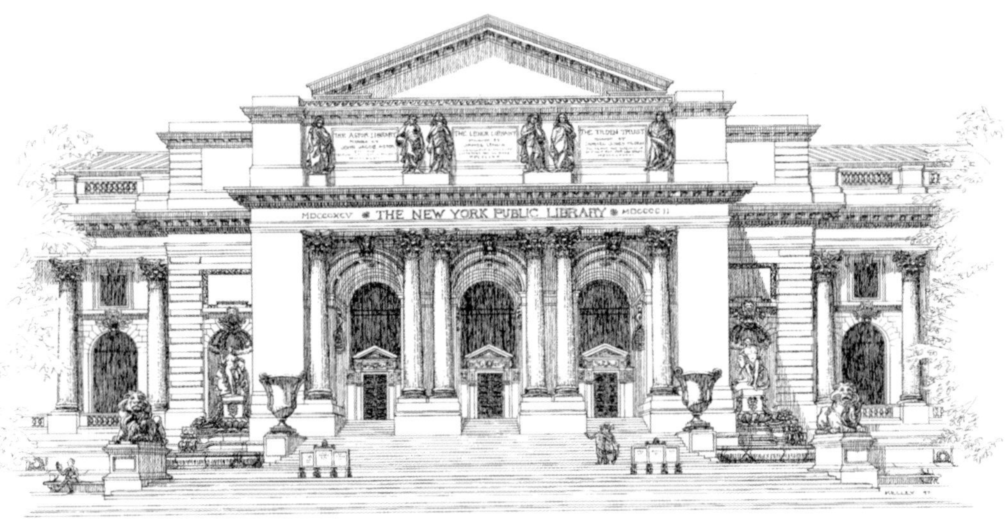

Illustration Credits

Tina Hoerenz: front cover, 1, 44–45, 71 below right; © Anne Day: 2, 3, 61 left, 62; © Peter Aaron/Esto: 4; Lis Pearson: 8; Photograph copyright © Jean-Marie Chauvet, Eliette Brunel Deschamps, and Christian Hillaire: 12 above; Maria Alos: 15; Courtesy of the Fairmount Park Art Association. Photograph: Howard Brunner © 1992: 17, 19 right; The Metropolitan Museum of Art, Rogers Fund, 1919 (19.127). Photograph, all rights reserved, The Metropolitan Museum of Art: 19 above left; Archives of The Pierpont Morgan Library, New York. ARC 1797. Photograph by Henry W. Louie: 19 below left; iStockphoto.com: 28; Courtesy of Bill Carroll and Mary Shelley. Originally published in *The American Magazine* (February 1930). Copy photograph by John Orth: 32; Courtesy of the Fragrance Foundation, New York, New York. Floral wreath by Gramercy Park Flower Shop. Photography by Sam Shahid: 39; Courtesy of Deborah DeSaix: 40; Courtesy of Peter Rose: 48; © 2006 Federated Department Stores, Inc.: 49 right; Courtesy of The Charles M. Daugherty Testamentary Trust. Used with permission of Viking Children's Books, a division of Penguin Group USA: 50–51; *The New Yorker,* © Condé Nast: 52 below, 64–65; © David Levine / *The New York Review of Books:* 53 above; © Dav Bordeleau: 53 below; © Jules Feiffer 2000: 54; Text and Art © 2005 by Carus Publishing Company. Reprinted by permission: 55; © The New Yorker Collection from cartoonbank.com. All Rights Reserved: 56 above, 58–59; Courtesy of Denys Wortman VIII: 56 below; © David M. Grossman: 60; © Don Hamerman: 61 right; Photographs by Debby Lee Cohen, All Rights Reserved ©: 63; © Peter Peirce: 69; © Al Hirschfeld, The Margo Feiden Galleries Ltd., New York: 71 left; © 2006 Artists Rights Society (ARS), New York/ADAGP, Paris: 72 left; Courtesy of SS+K, New York: 73 below; Courtesy of the Estate of Tony Sarg: 74; © Stan Lichens: 75 above; Courtesy of Mildred Merrick: 75 below left; Ben Asen ©: 75 below right; Courtesy of Helen and Will Levine: 80.

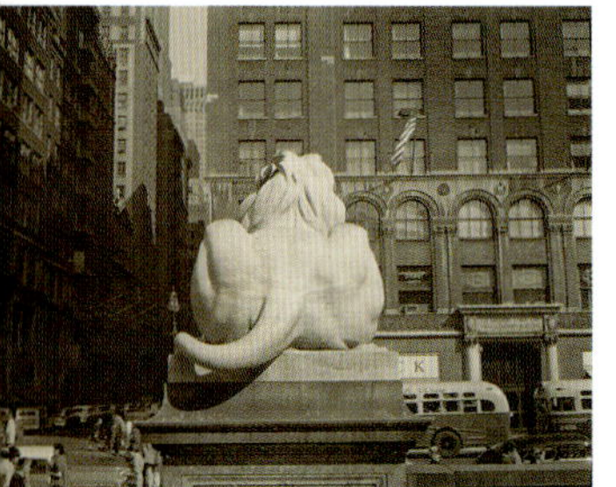

Sy Seidman. *Rear View of the South Library Lion.* Photograph, 1955.

New York Public Library Collections

NYPL collections represented in *Top Cats* include the Mid-Manhattan Picture Collection (MMPC) and the following collections of the Humanities and Social Sciences Library: the Asian and Middle Eastern Division (AME); the General Research Division (GRD); The Irma and Paul Milstein Division of United States History, Local History and Genealogy (LHG); the Microforms Section (MIC); the Manuscripts and Archives Division (MSS); the New York Public Library Archives (NYPLA); the Photography Collection (PHG) and the Print Collection (PRN) of The Miriam and Ira D. Wallach Division of Art, Prints and Photographs; and the Spencer Collection (SPN). NYPL's Public Relations Office (PRO) also contributed to this volume.

AME: 11 (Herbert C. White, *Peking the Beautiful.* Shanghai, 1927), 12 below (Austen Henry Layard, *A Second Series of the Monuments of Nineveh.* London, 1853).

GRD: 10 and 21 above (*Picturesque World's Fair.* Chicago, 1894), 21 below (*Report, Transmitted to the Legislature April 18, 1894.* Albany, 1894), 30, 37, 40, 58 left and right, 71 above right.

LHG: 74.

MIC: 52 above and below, 53 above, 73 above.

MMPC: 13 above (August-Charles-Joseph Vitu, *450 dessins inédits d'après nature.* Paris, 1889), 13 below.

MSS, Edward Clark Potter Papers: 16, 20, 24, 25.

MSS, New Yorker Covers Collection: 64–65.

NYPLA: 9 and 46, 22, 26 and 34 (Photographs by A. E. Sproul), 35, 48, 49 right, 66, 72 left, 73 below, 75 below right, 76.

PHG: 49 left, 67 (Published in the *Bulletin* of The New York Public Library, Vol. 47, No. 3 [March 1943], between pp. 136 and 137), 68 above and below, 80.

PRN: 47, 56 above and below, 59, 70, 71 left, 72 right, 75 below left.

PRO: 2, 3, 4, 8, 18 and back cover, 20, 39, 43, 44–45, 52, 53 below, 54–55, 57, 60–63, 69, 78–79.

SPN: 50, 51 above and below.